Colorful Country Painted Coloring Book

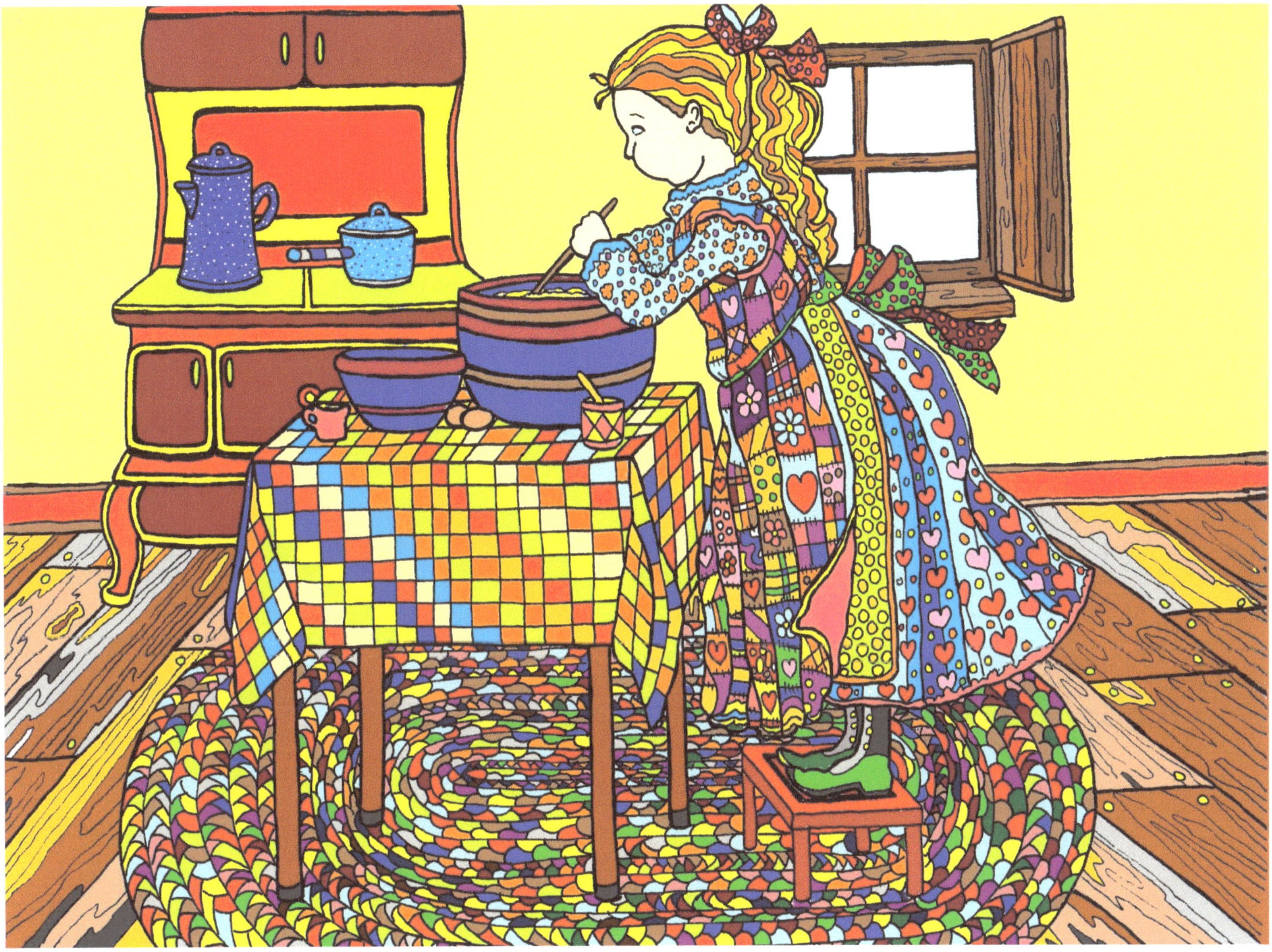

Colorful Country Painted Coloring Book, Colored Coloring Volume 2

Copyrights 2018© Lauri Ann Kraft

All rights reserved

Permission to post copies of my artwork

online as part of a book review.

WWW.COLORWYOMING.COM

WWW.FACEBOOK.COM/KRAFTSART

ISBN-13: 978-1987532500

COLORFUL COLORING

Made in the USA

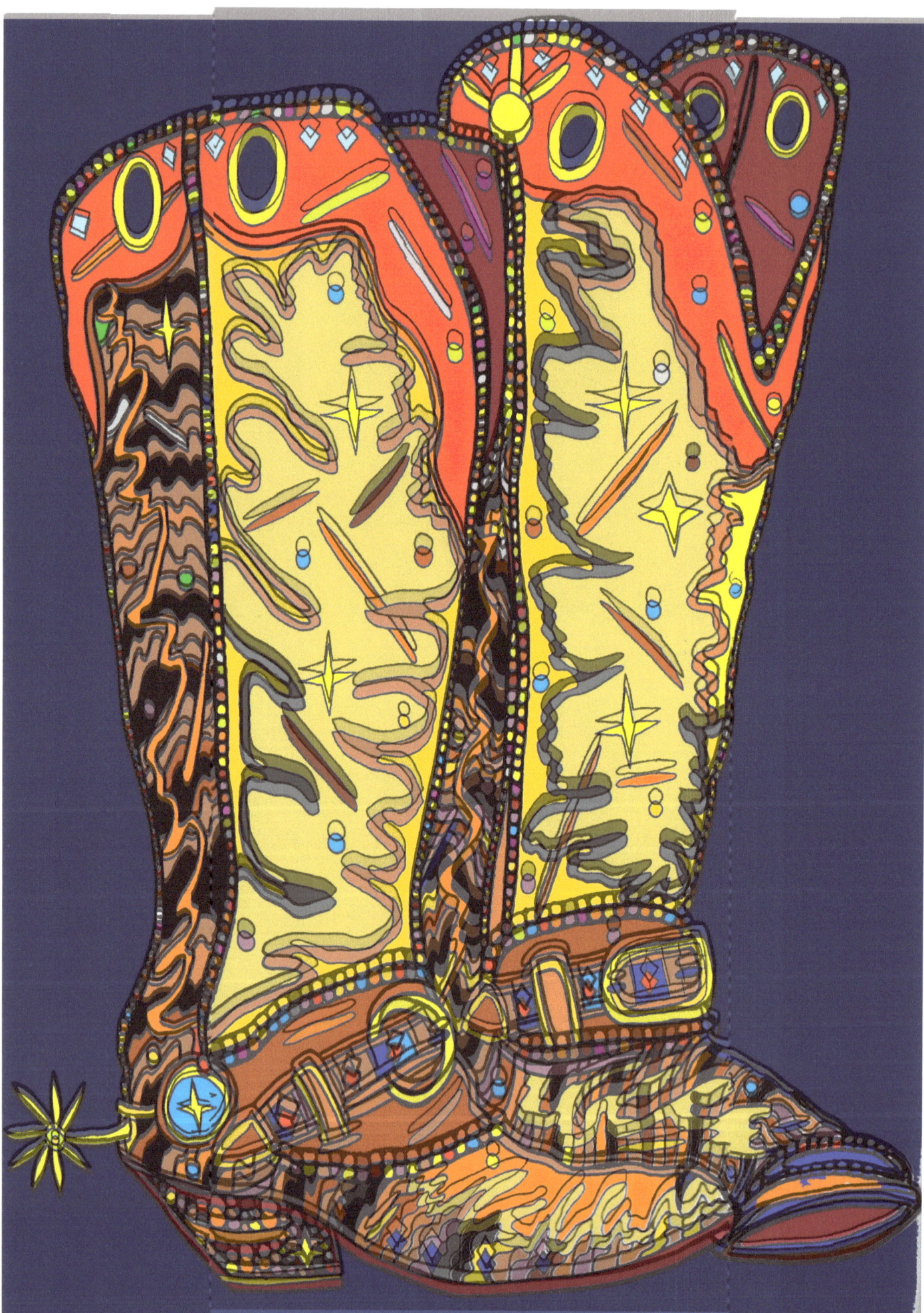

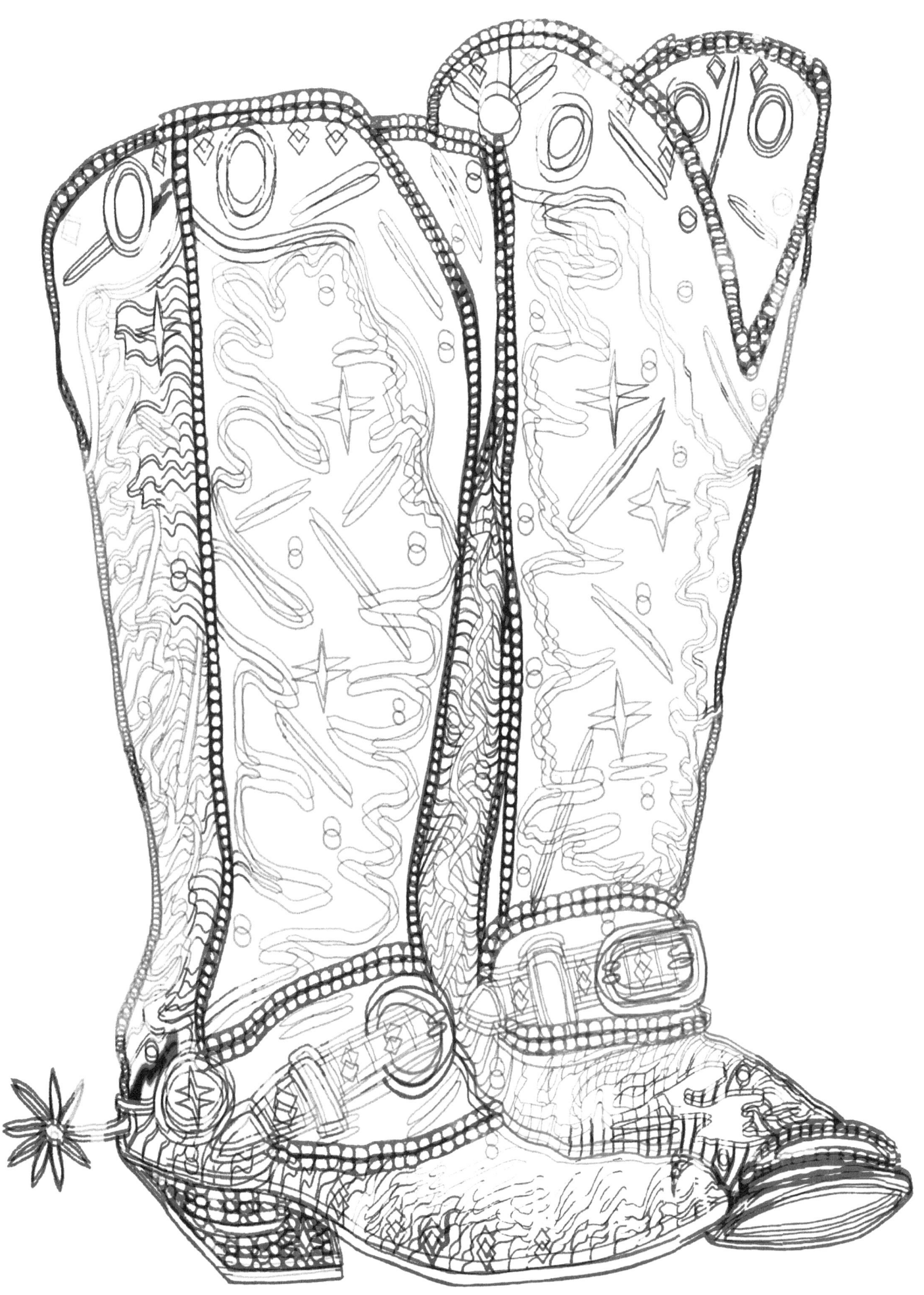

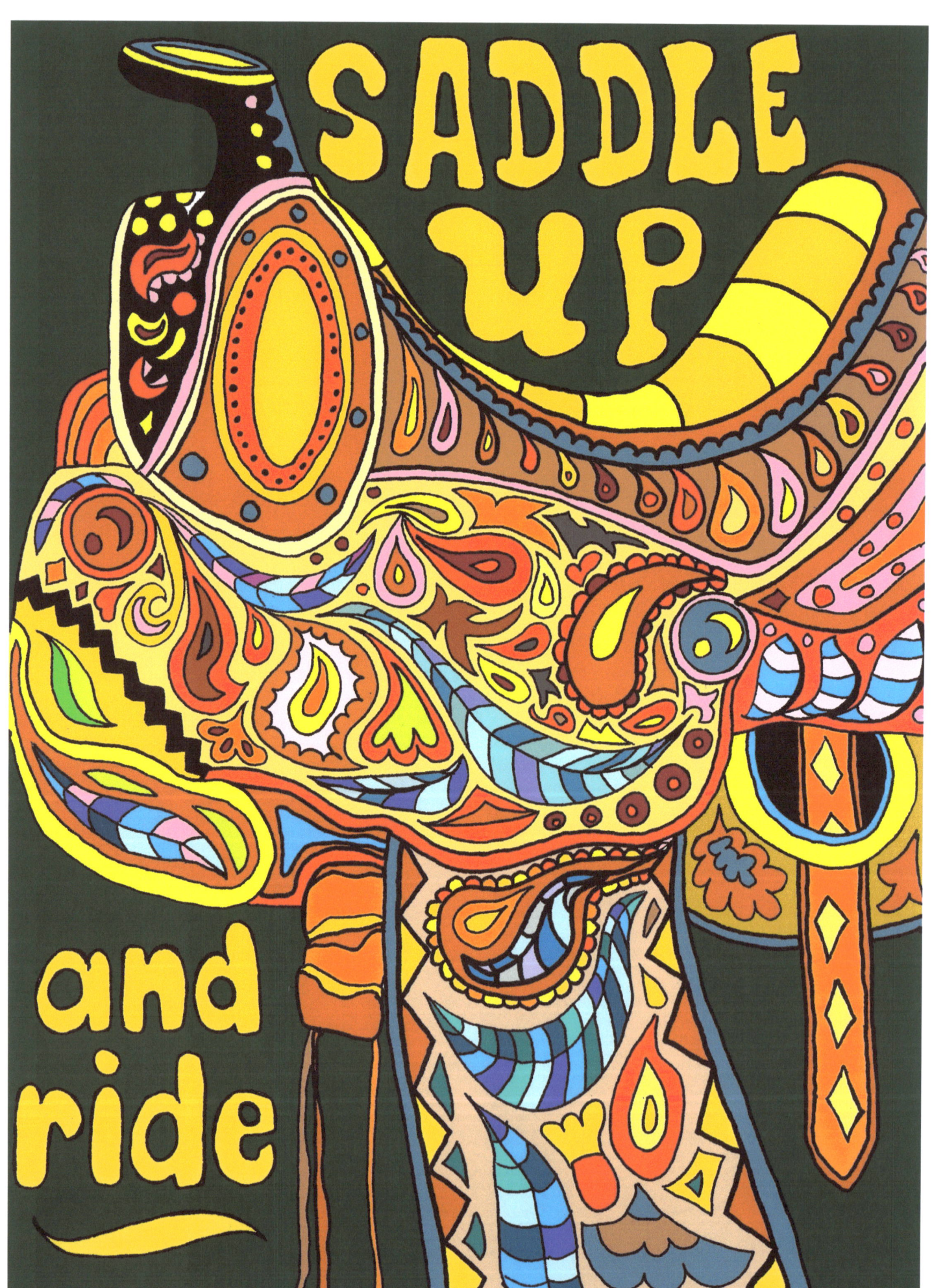

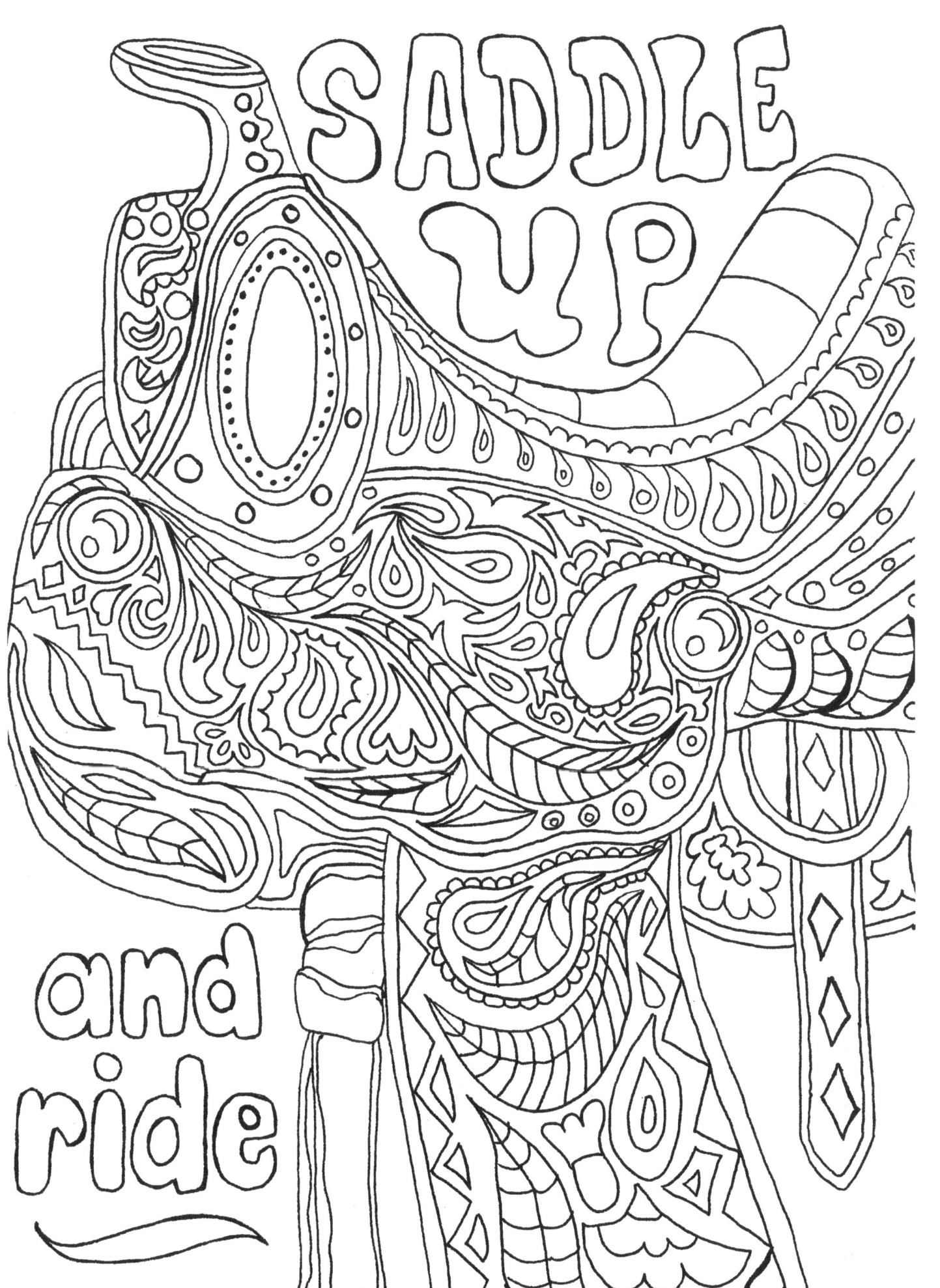

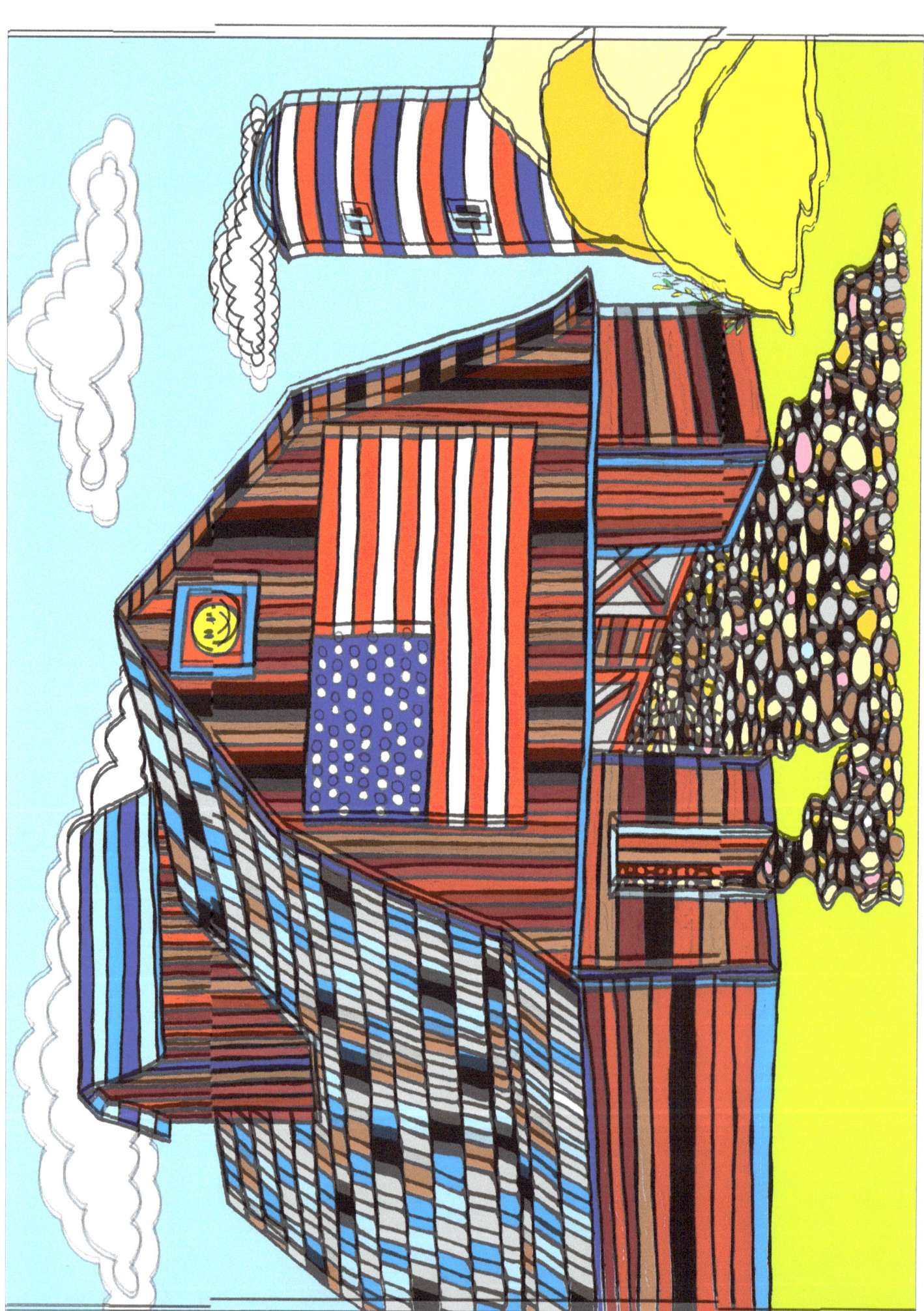

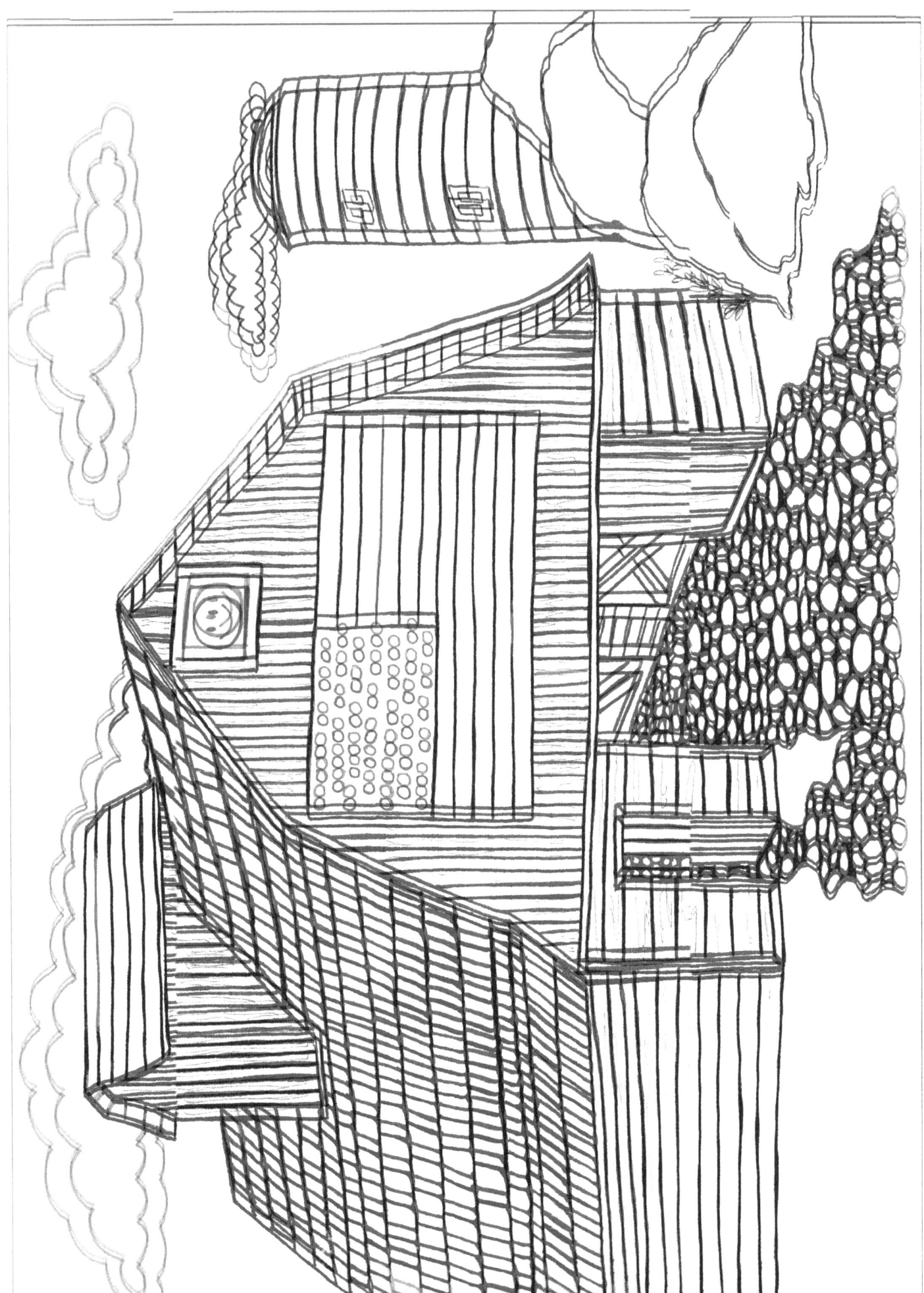

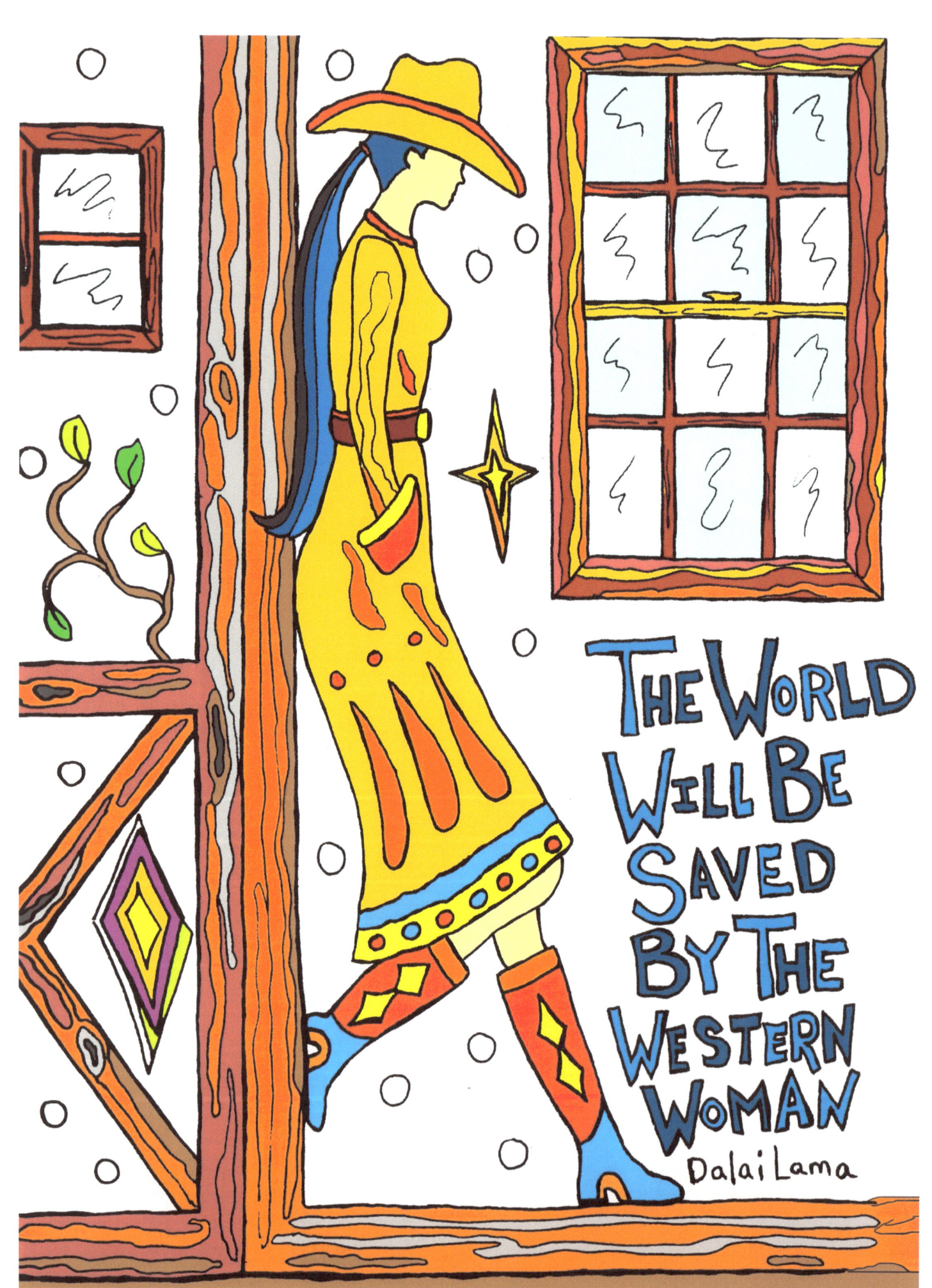

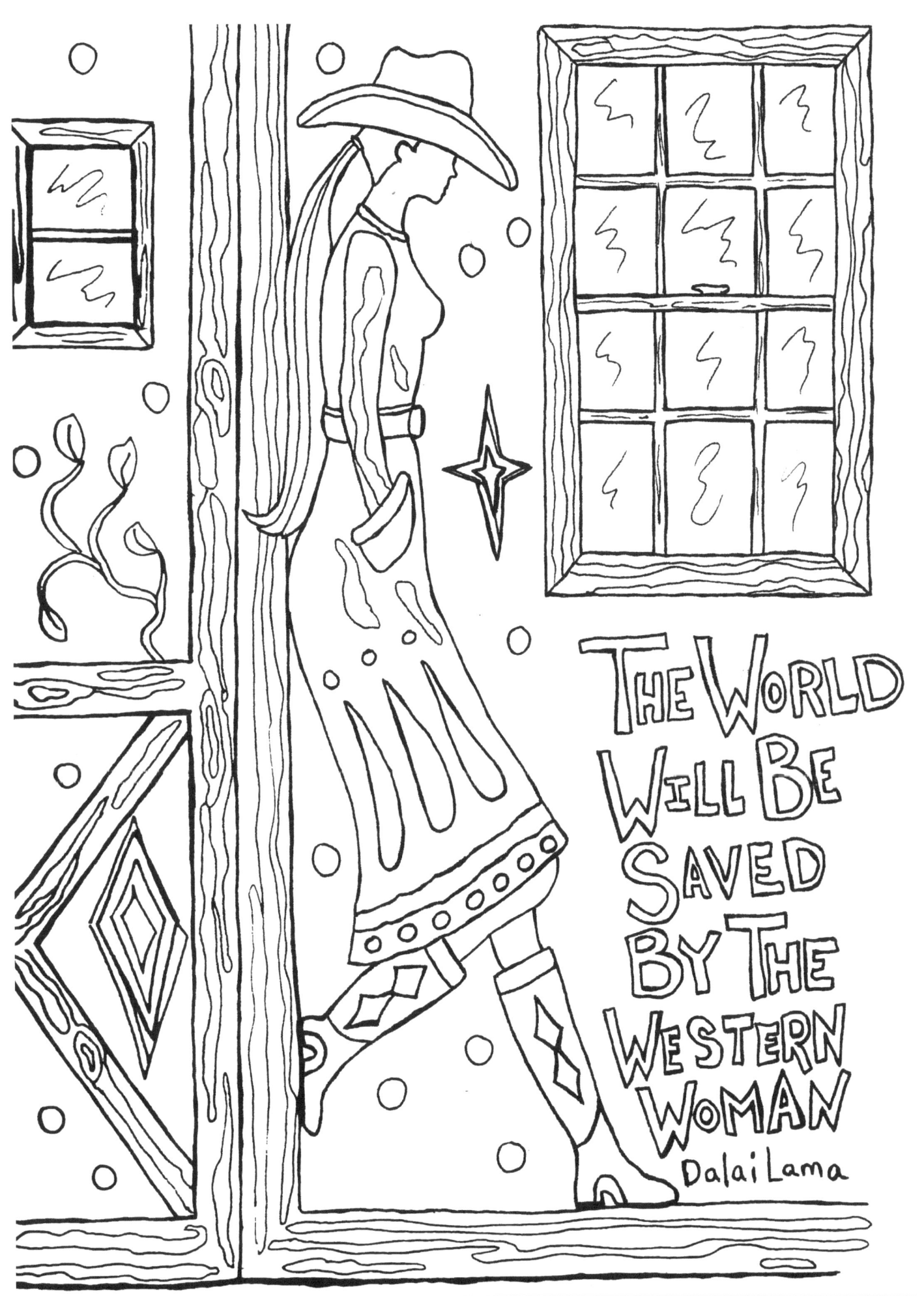

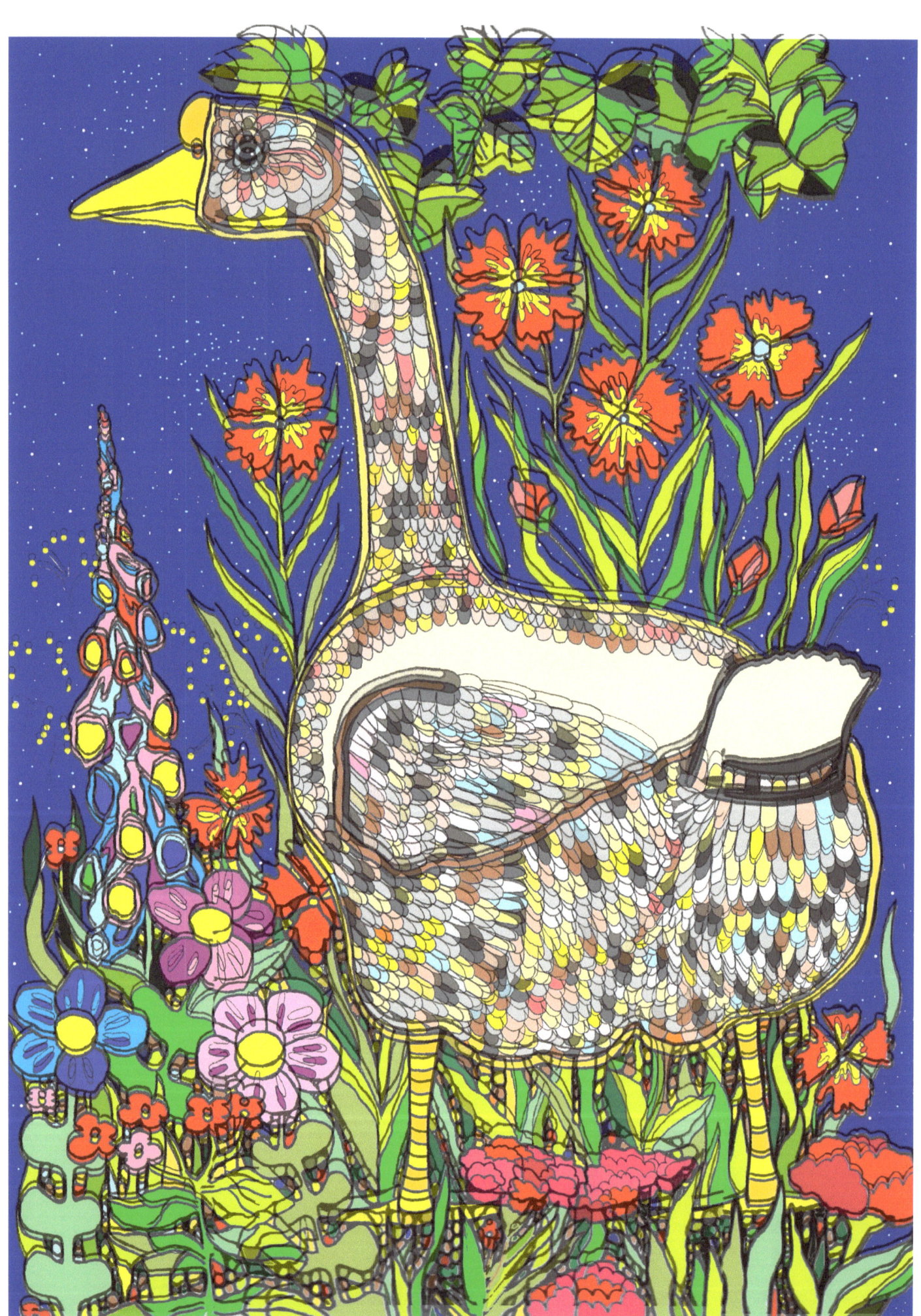

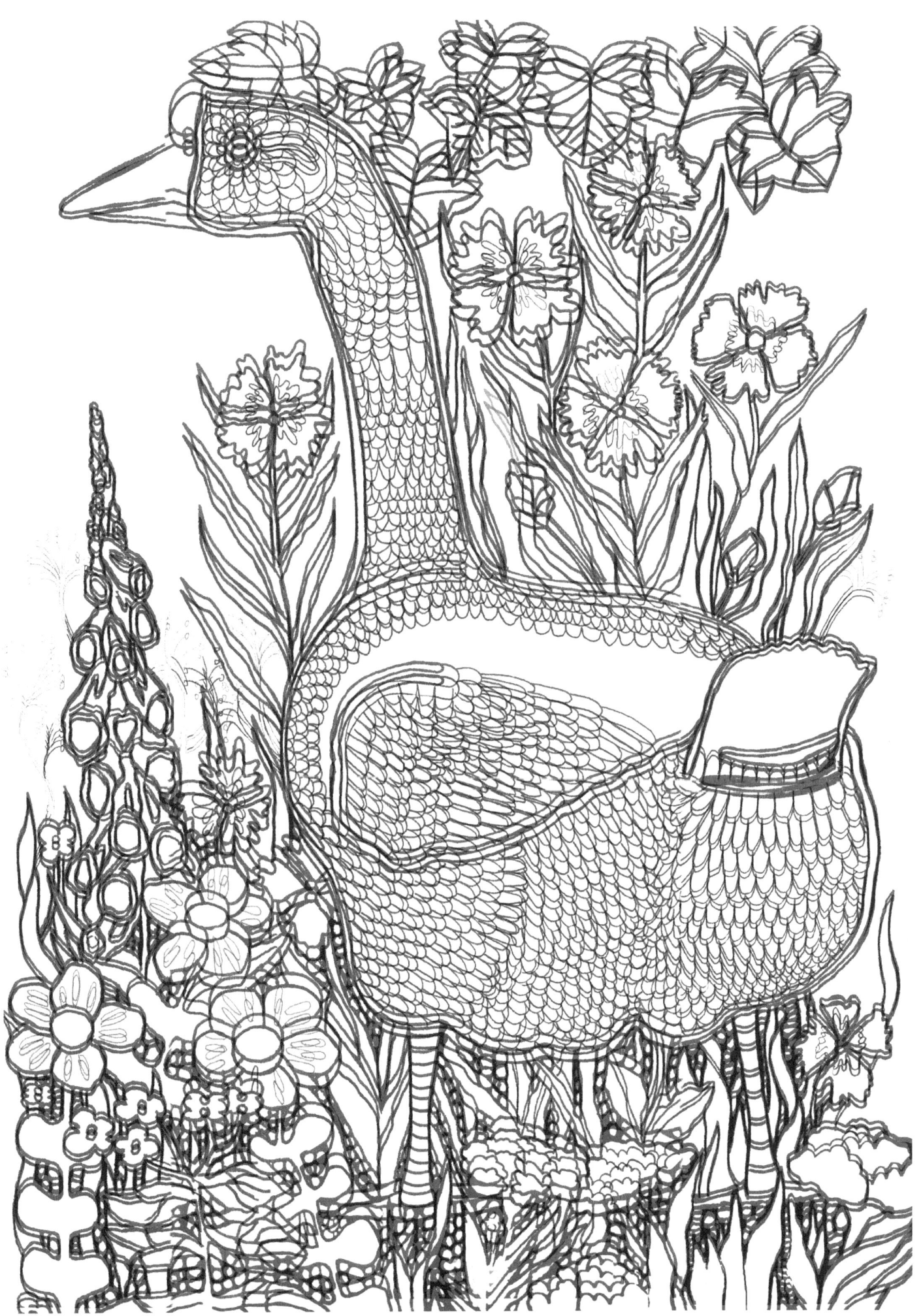

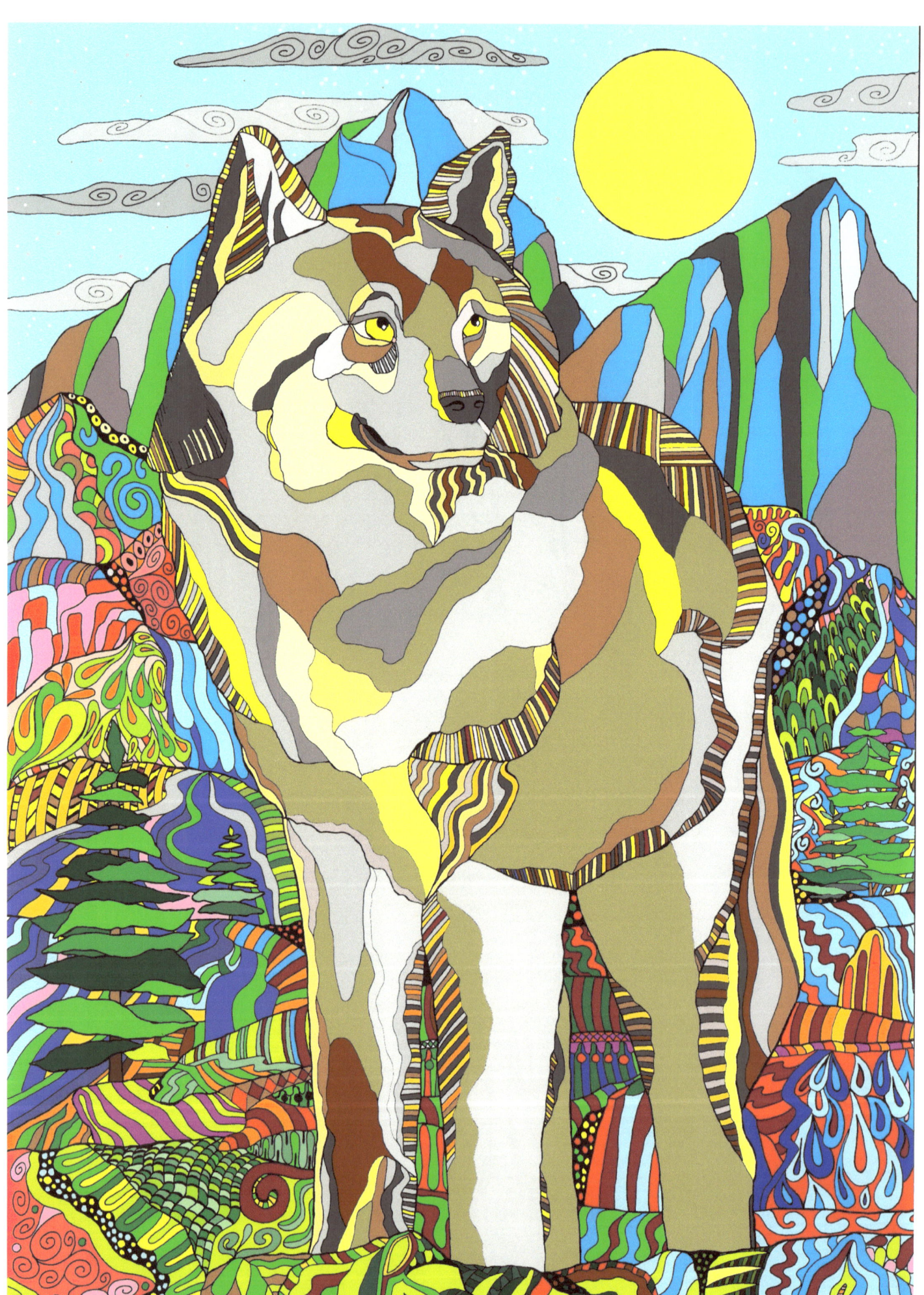

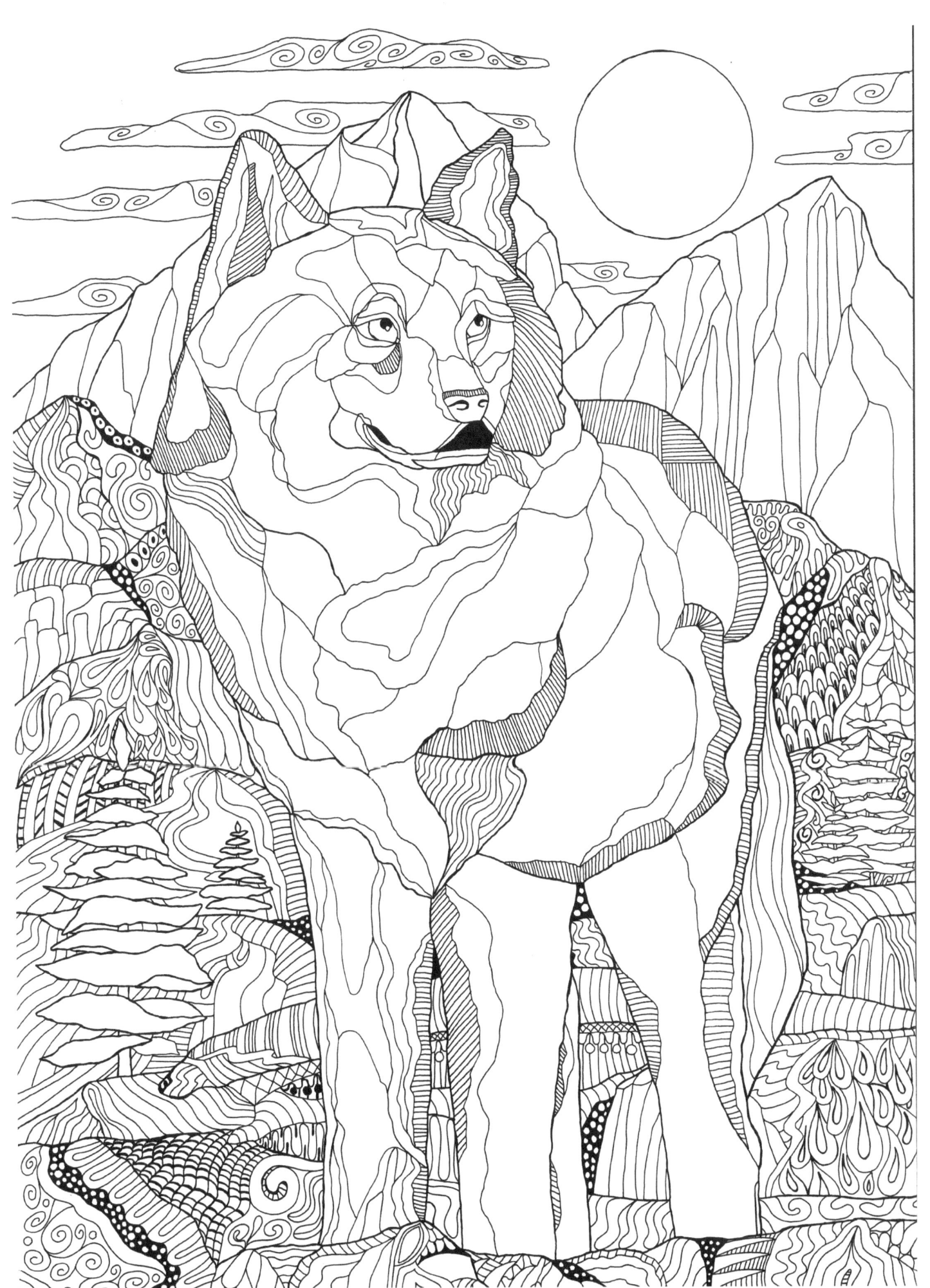

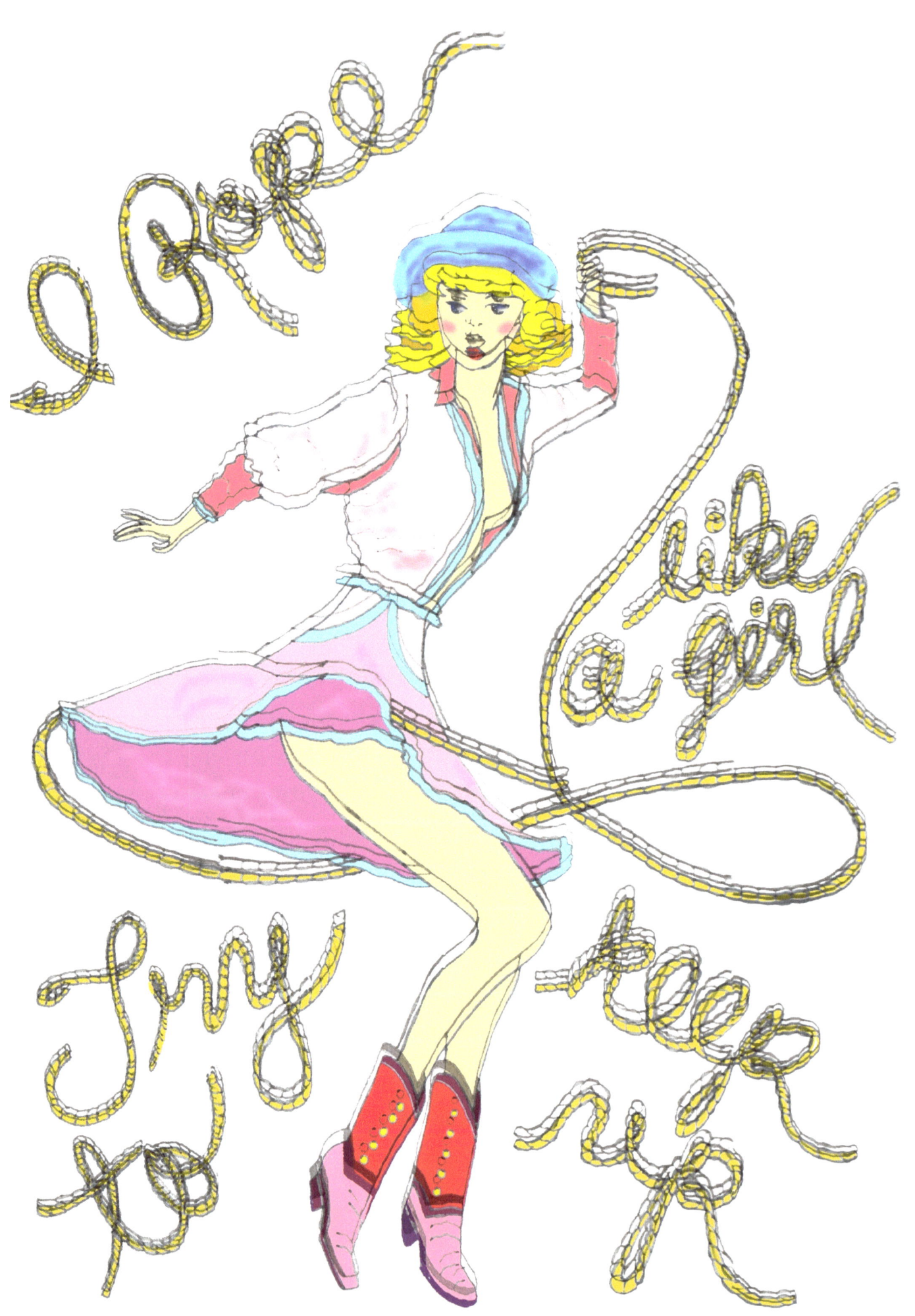

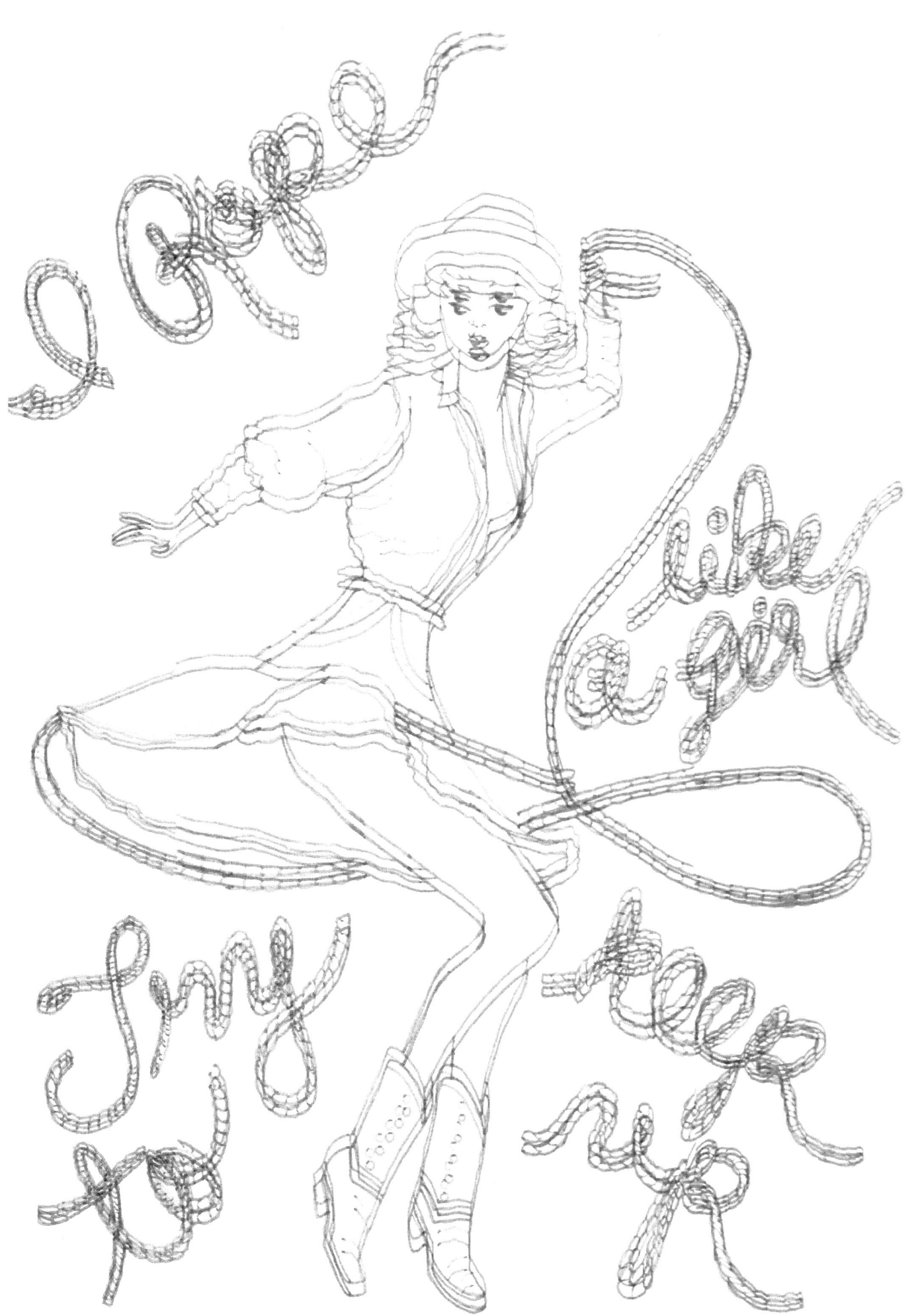

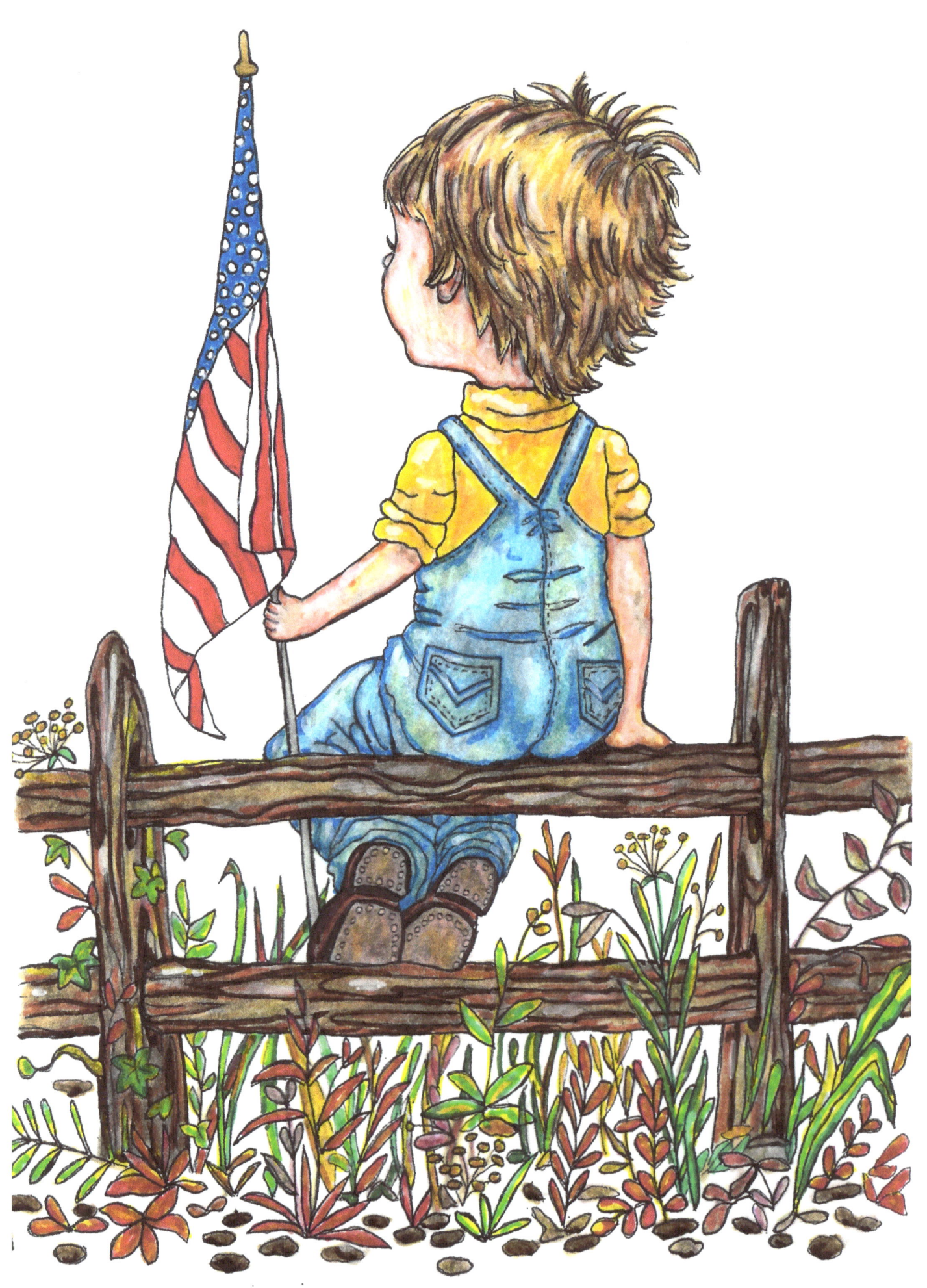

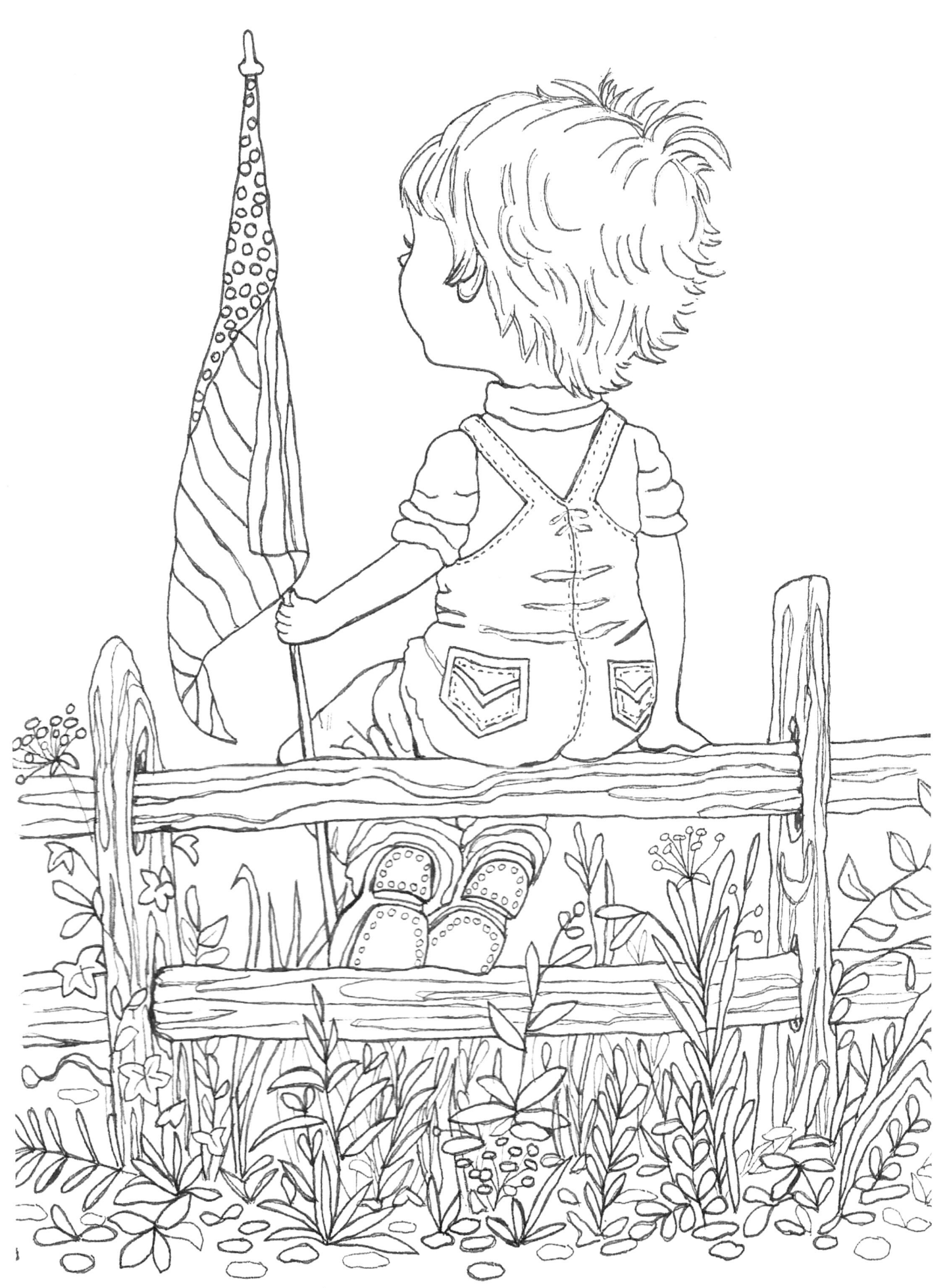

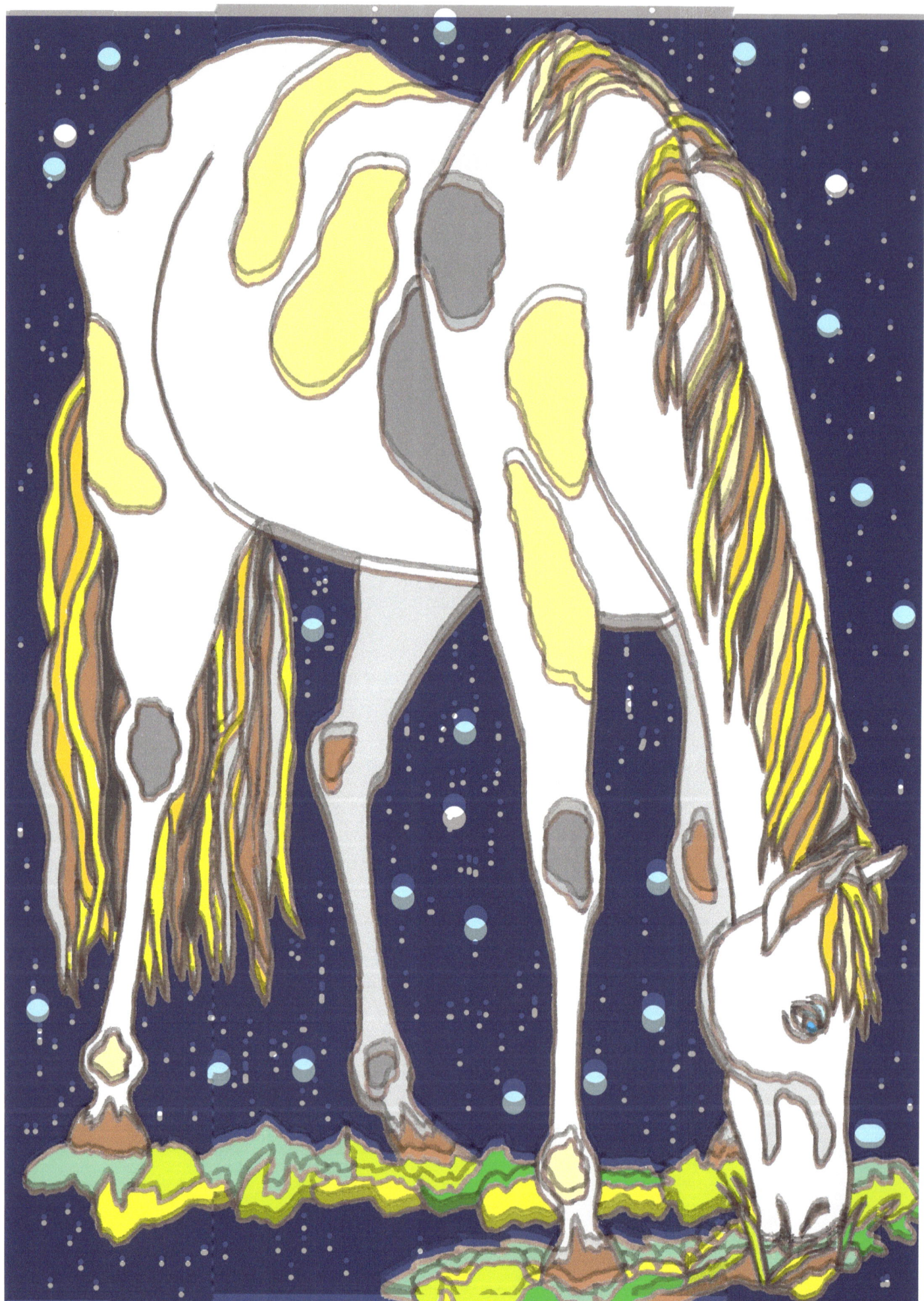

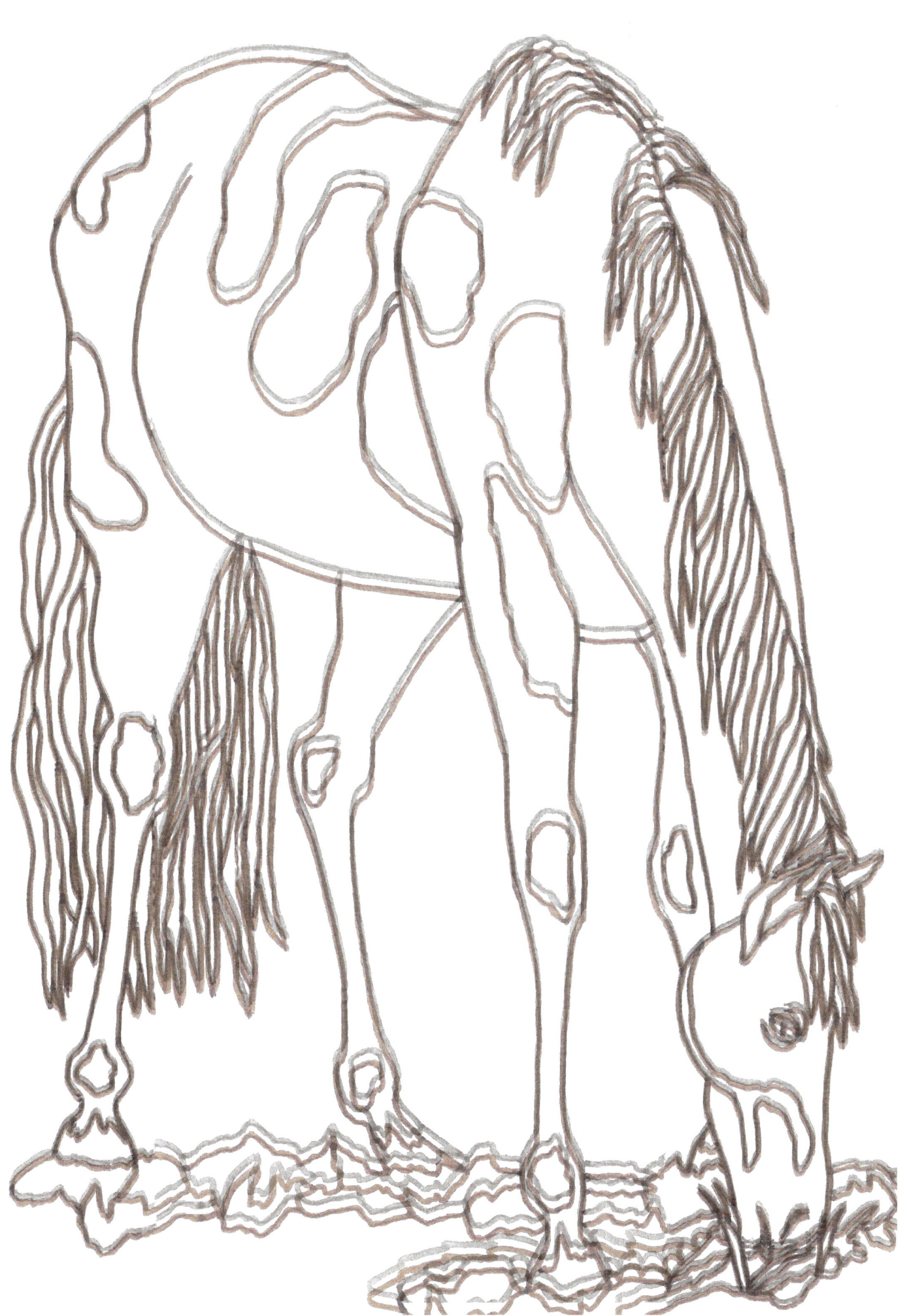

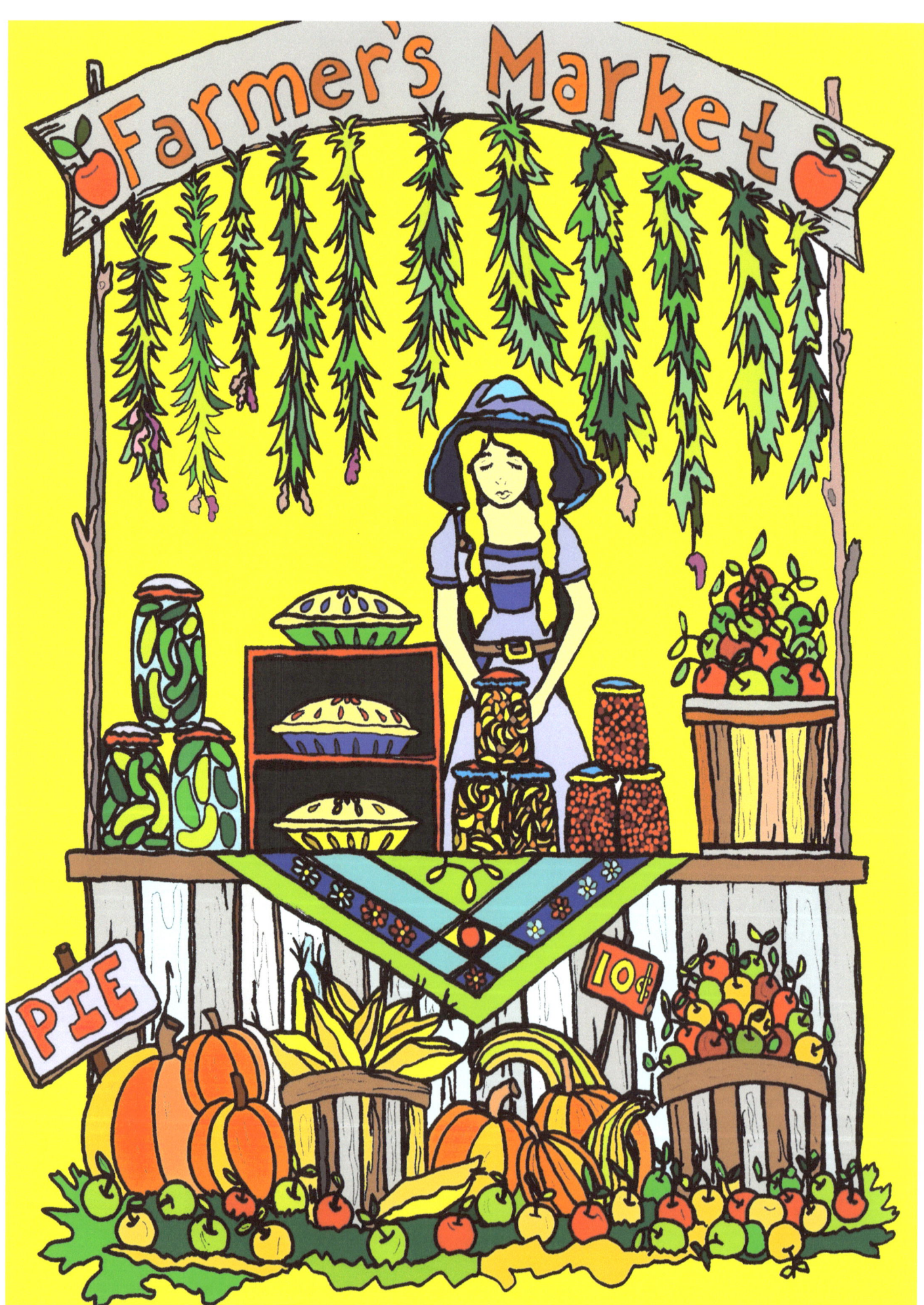

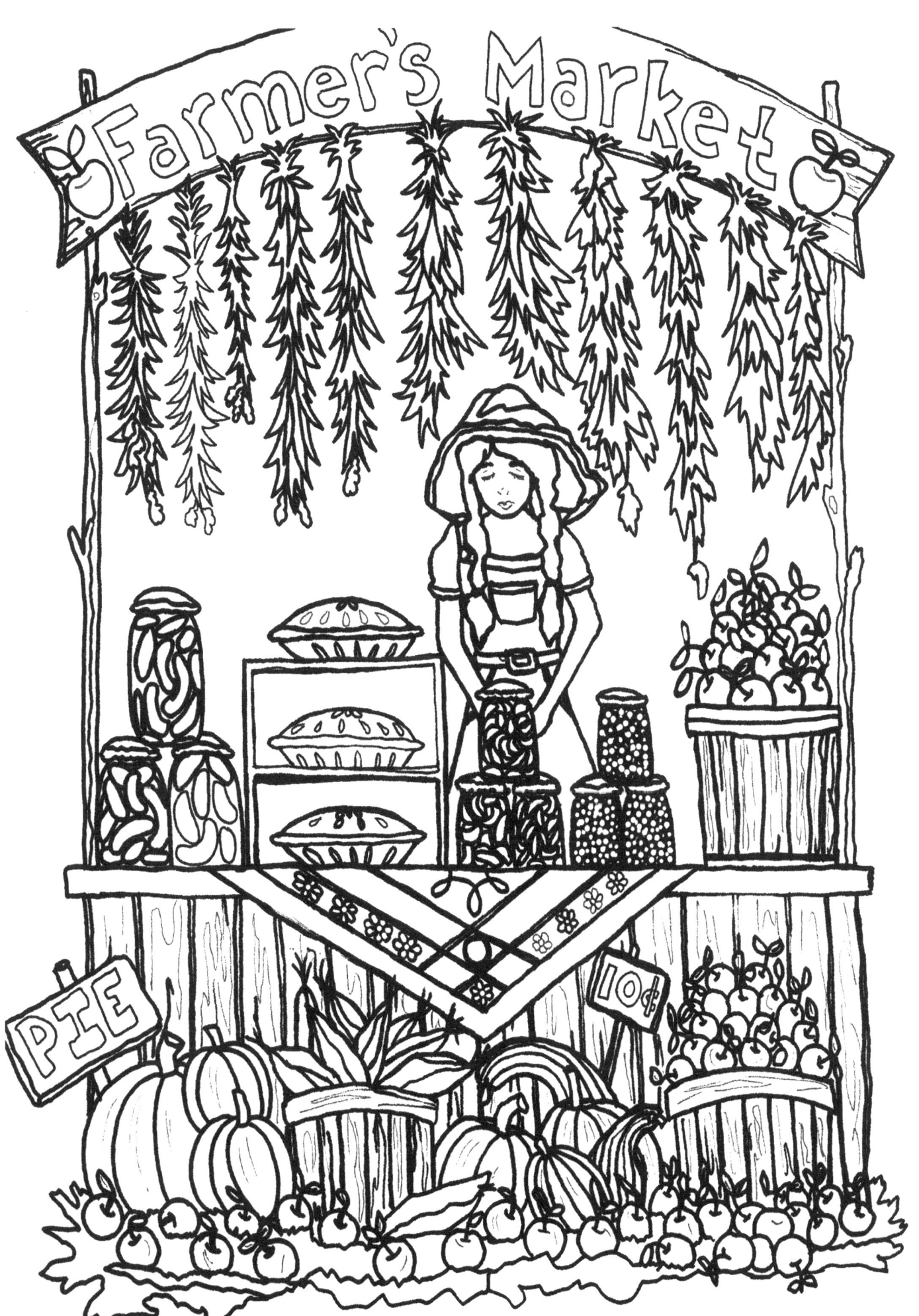

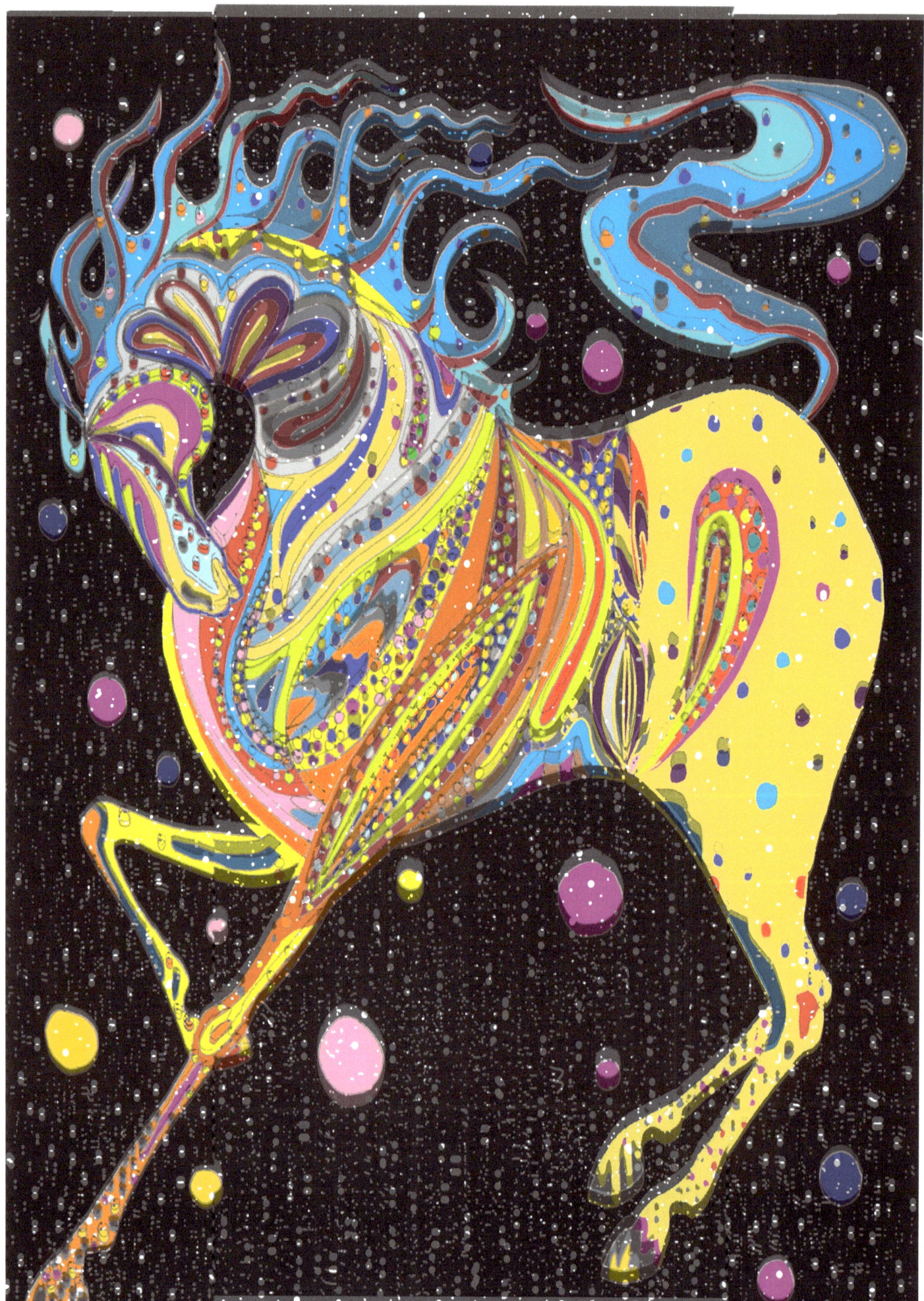

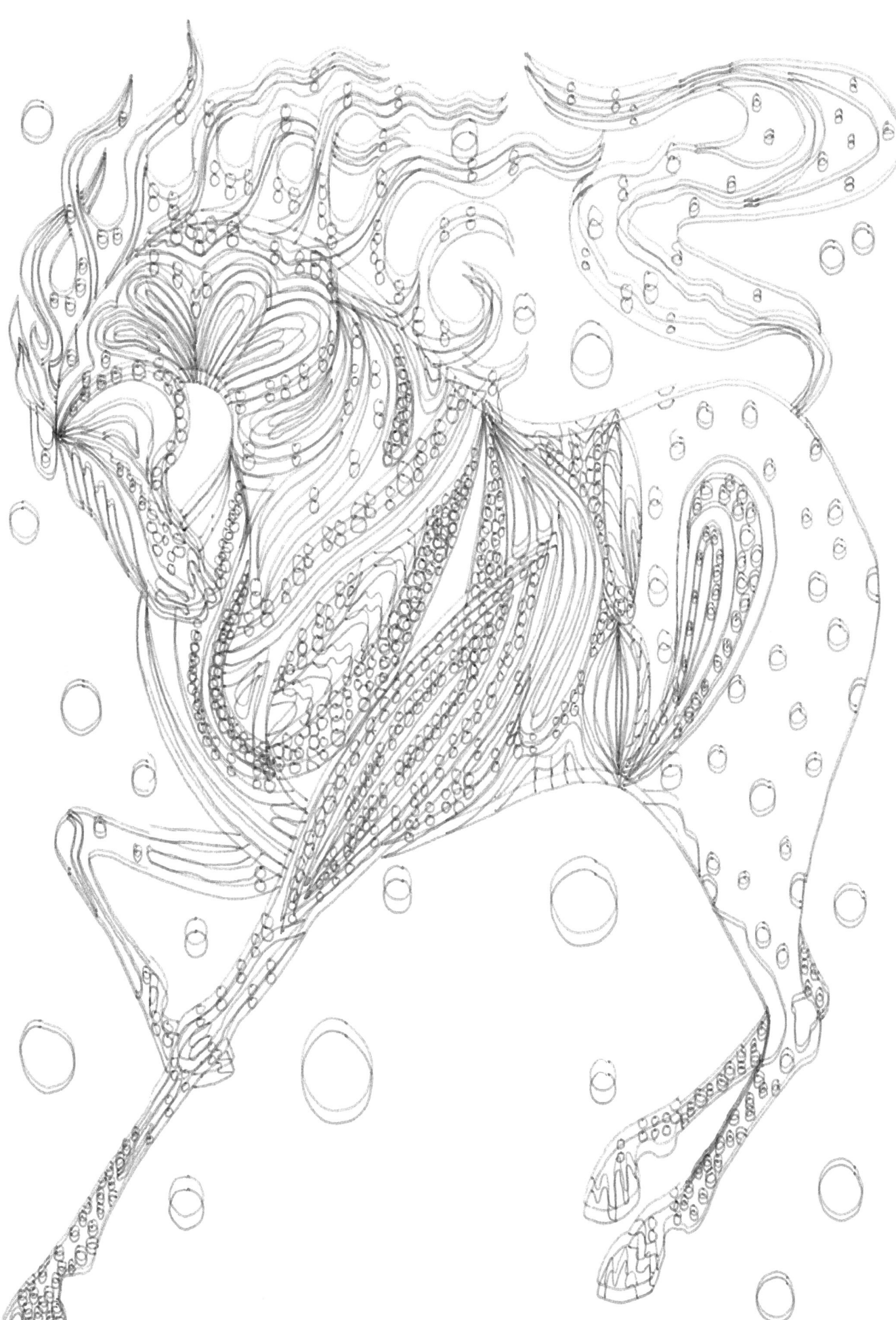

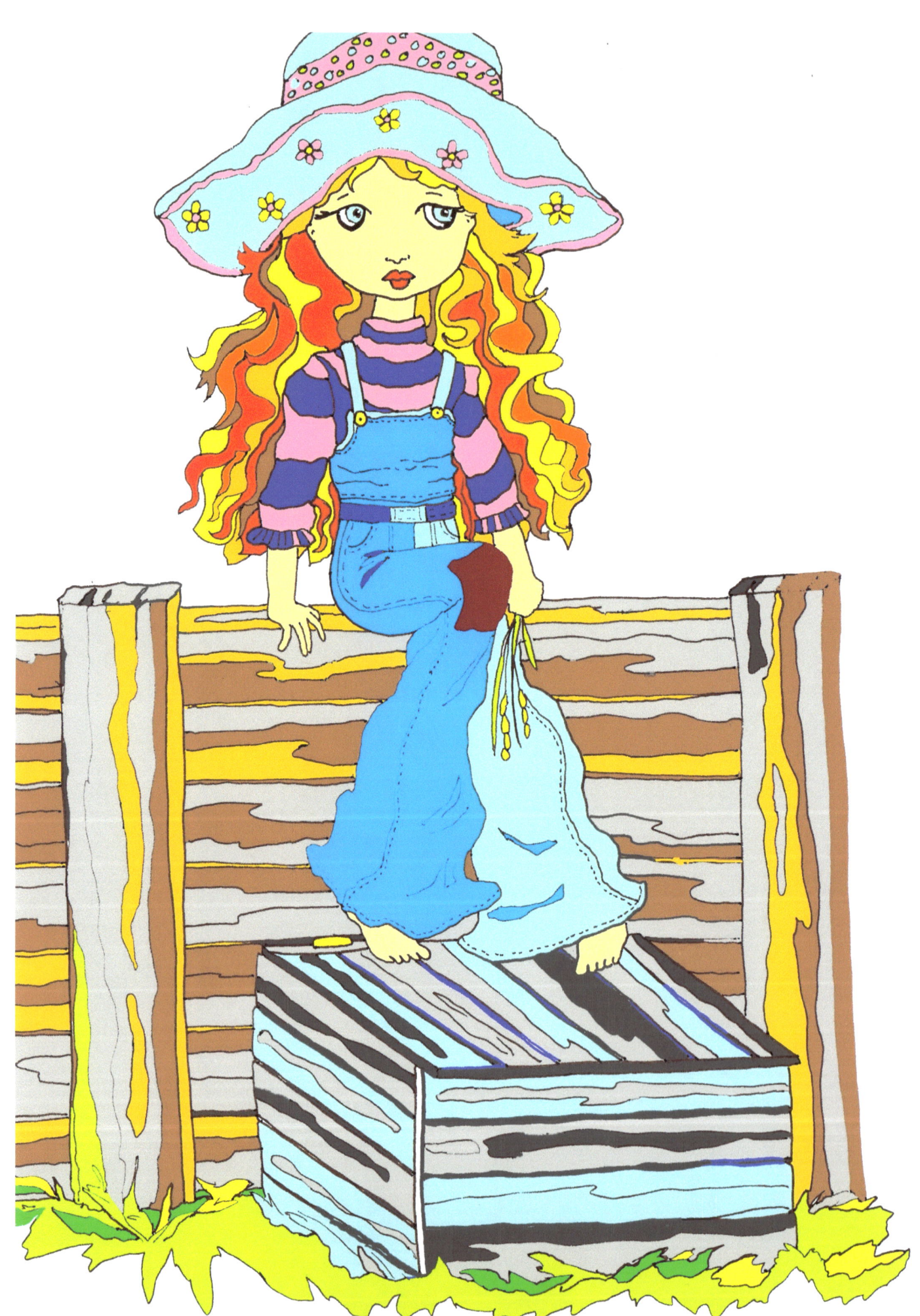

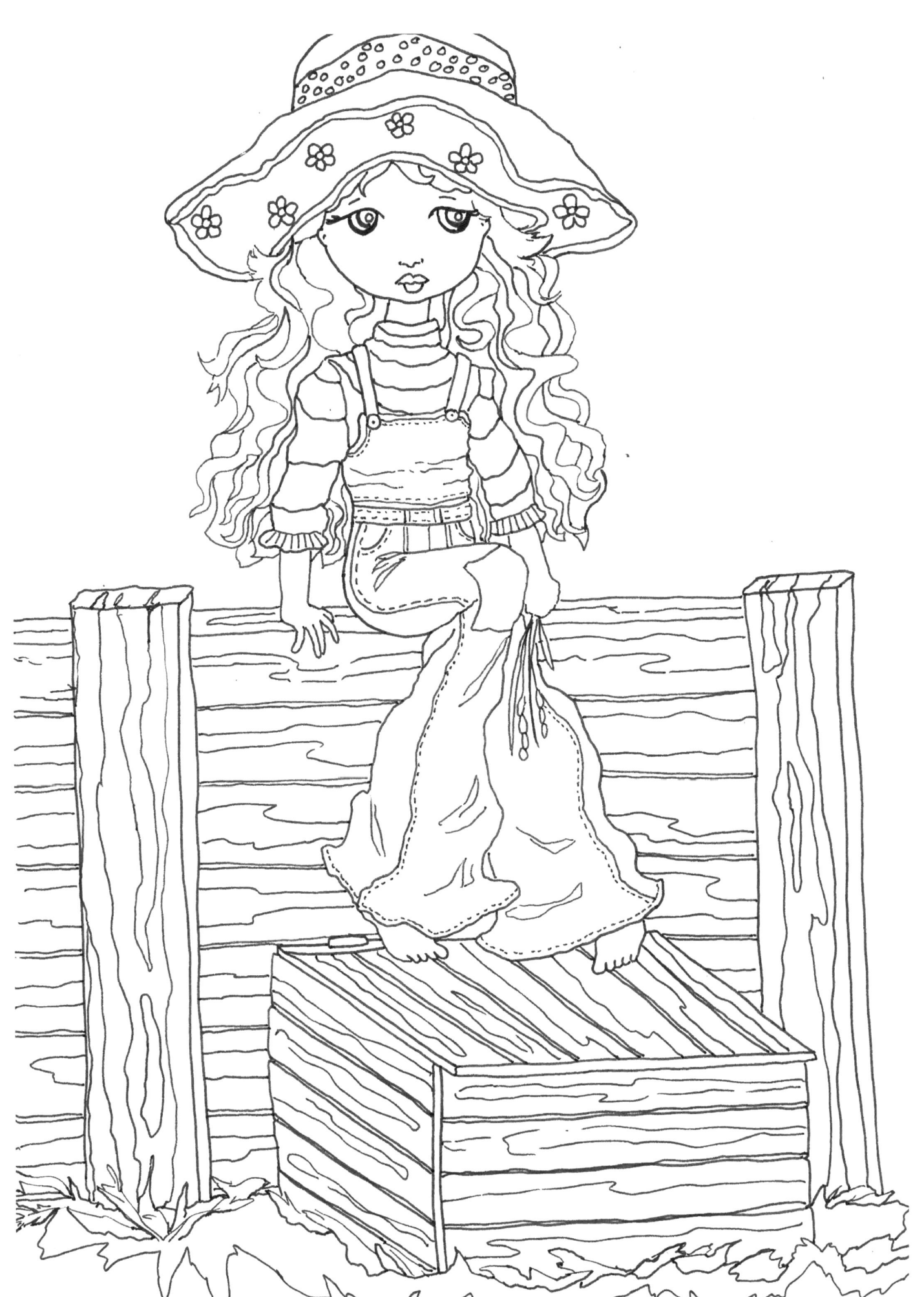

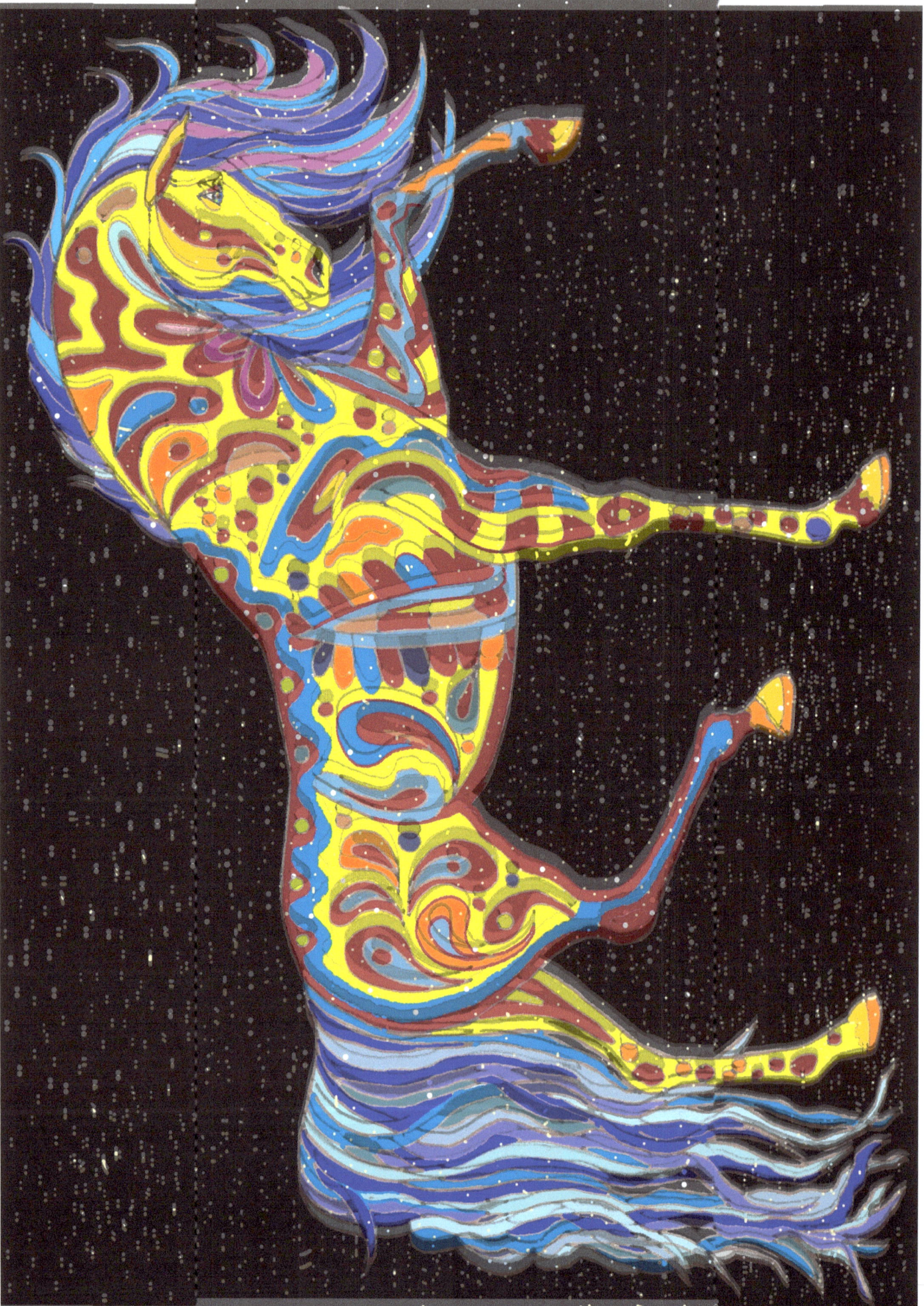

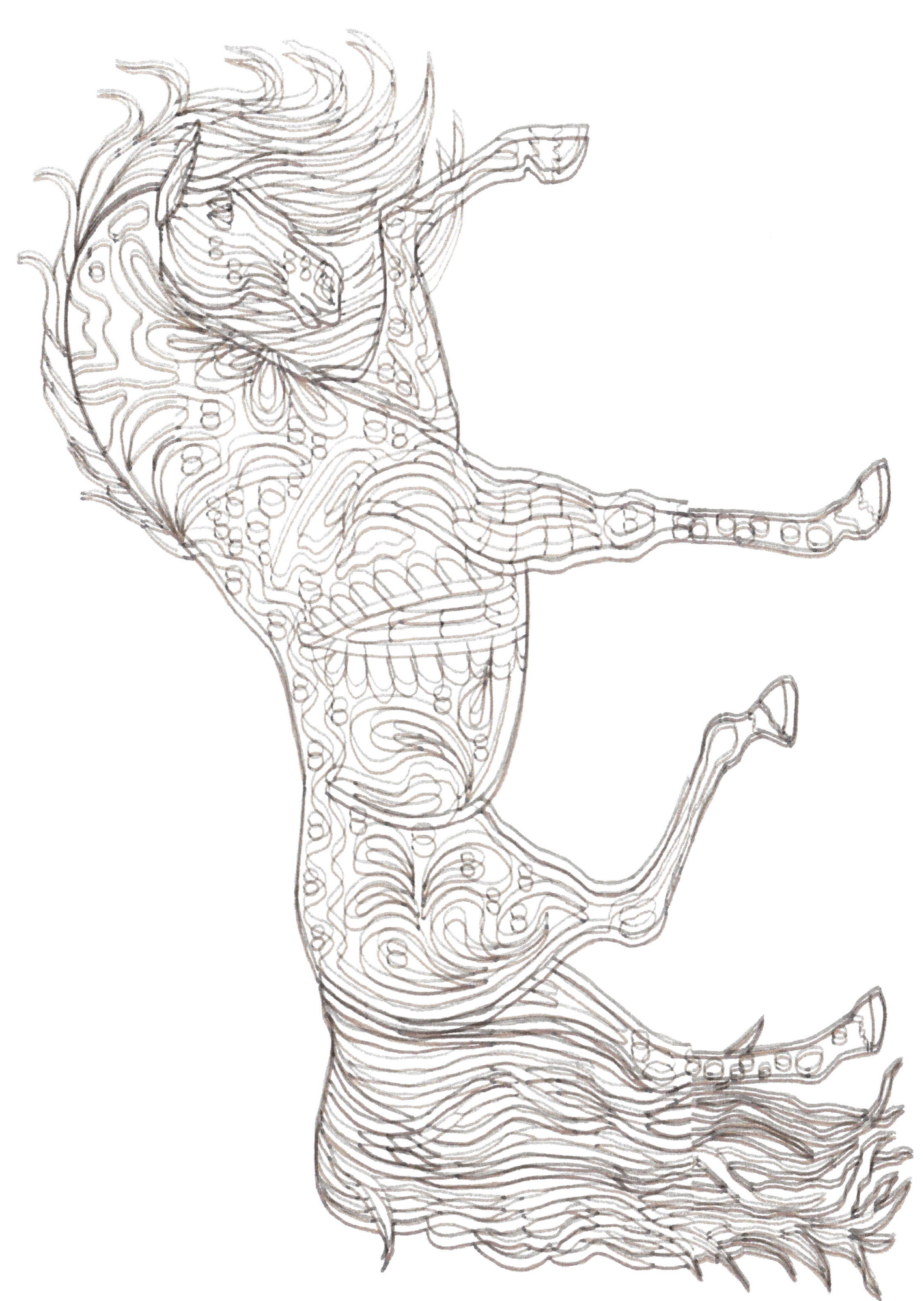

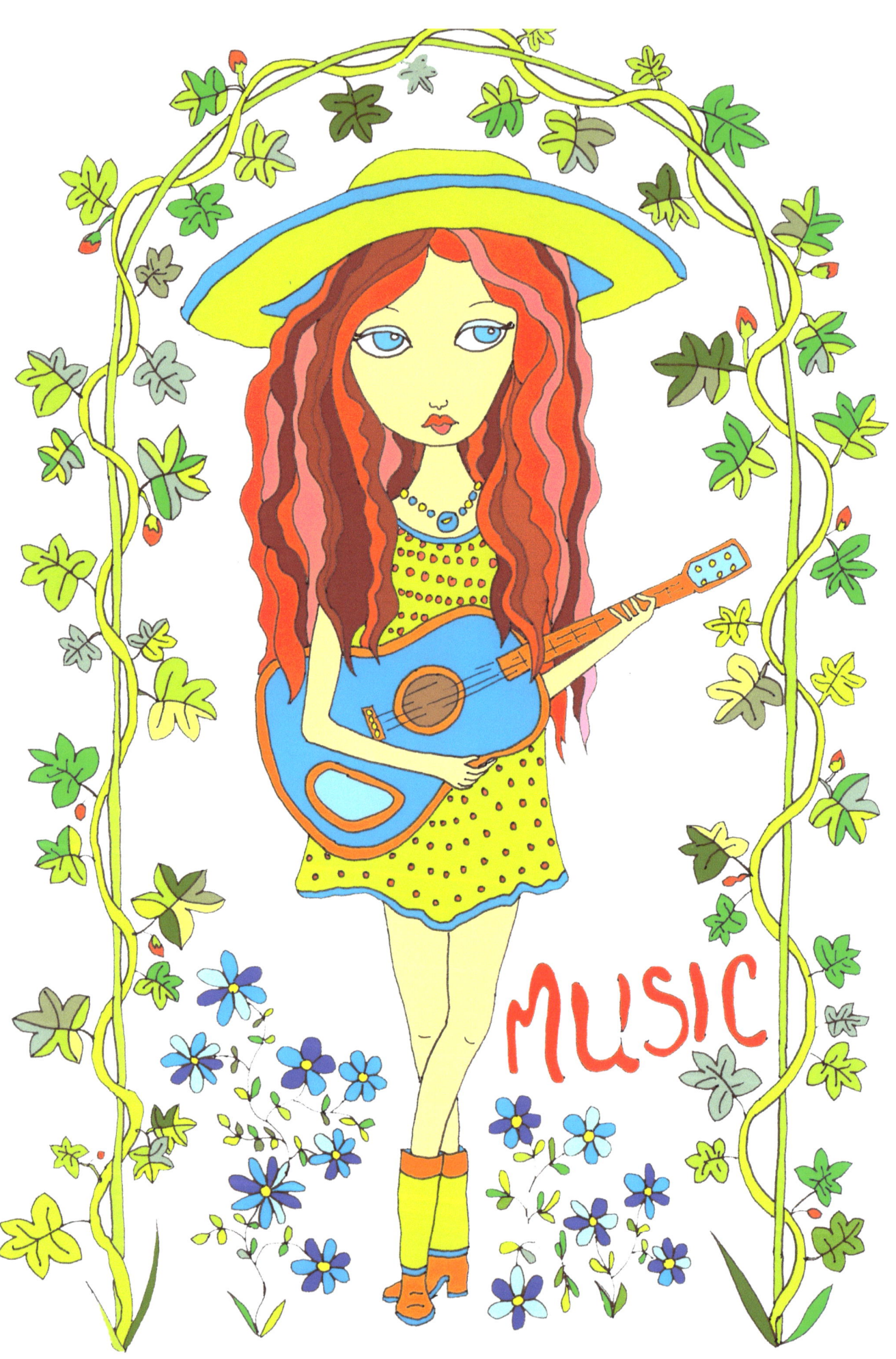

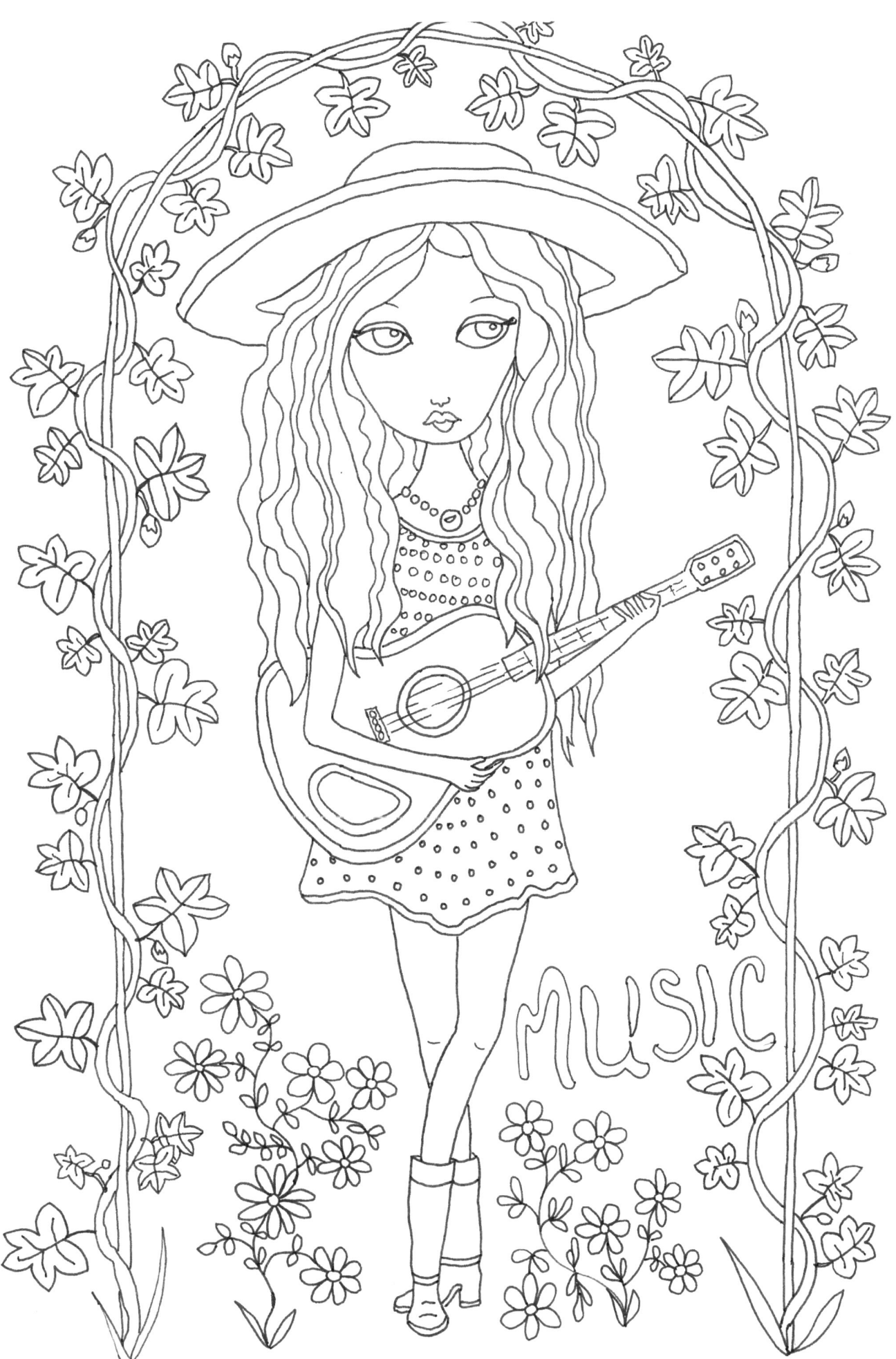

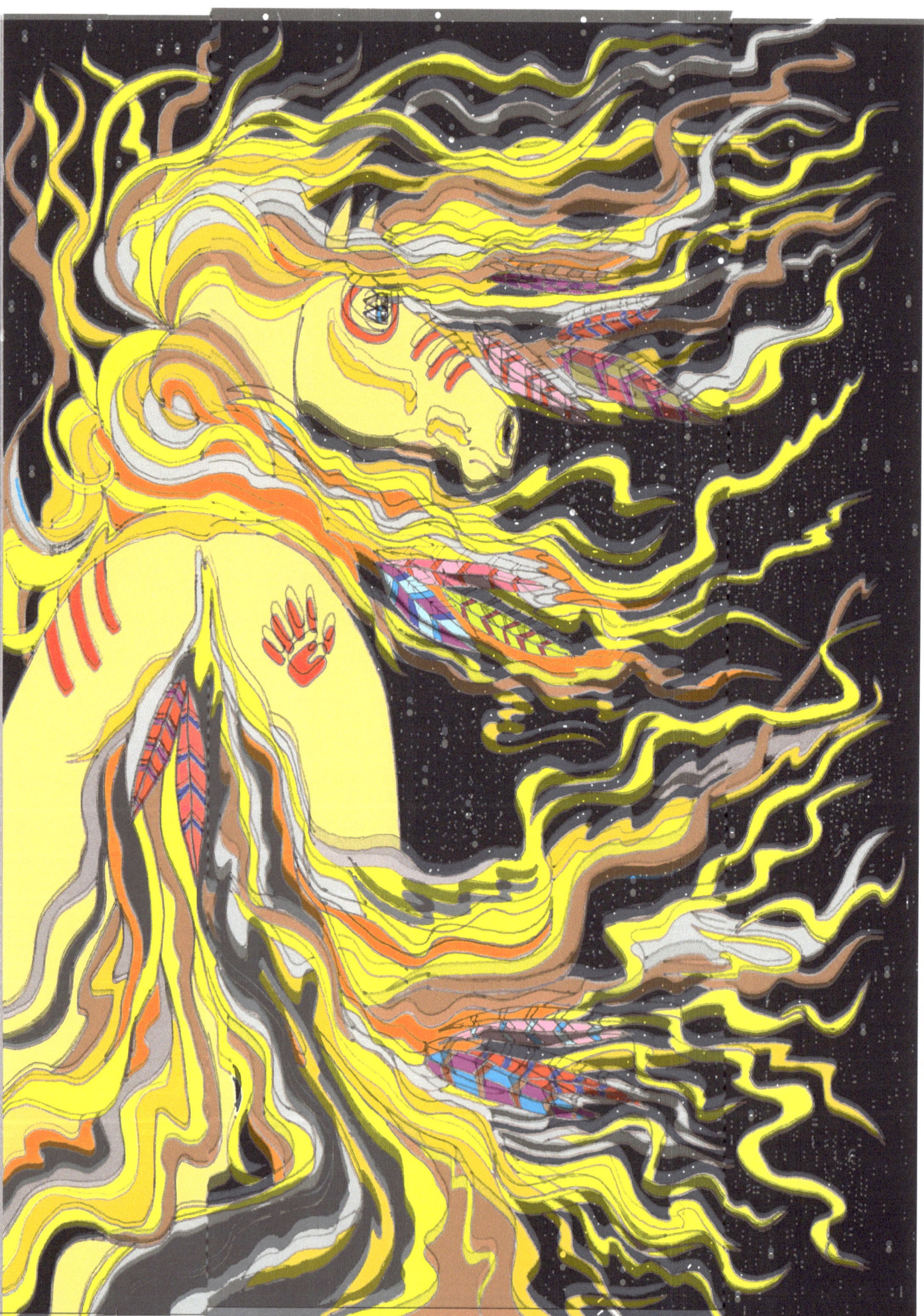

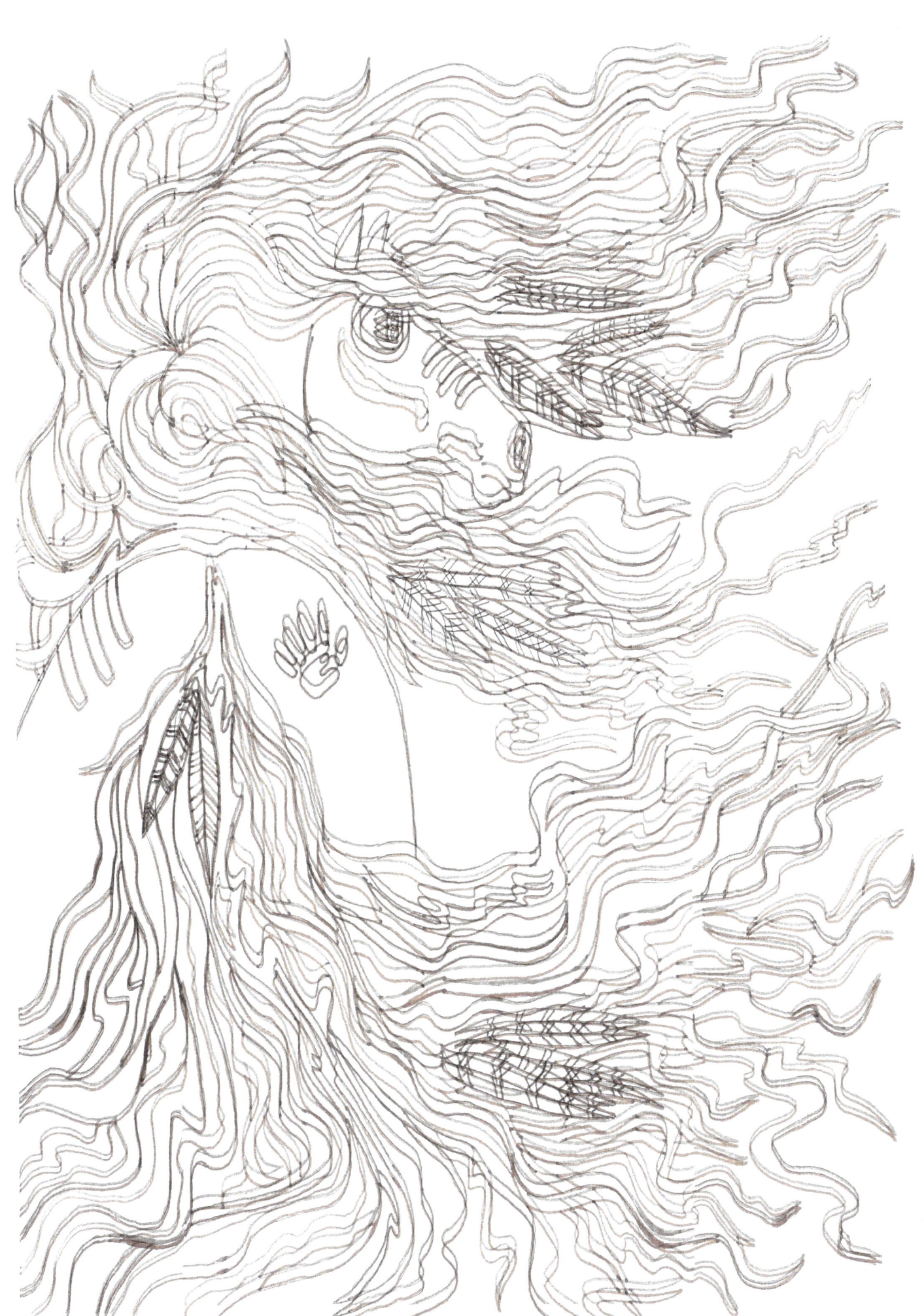

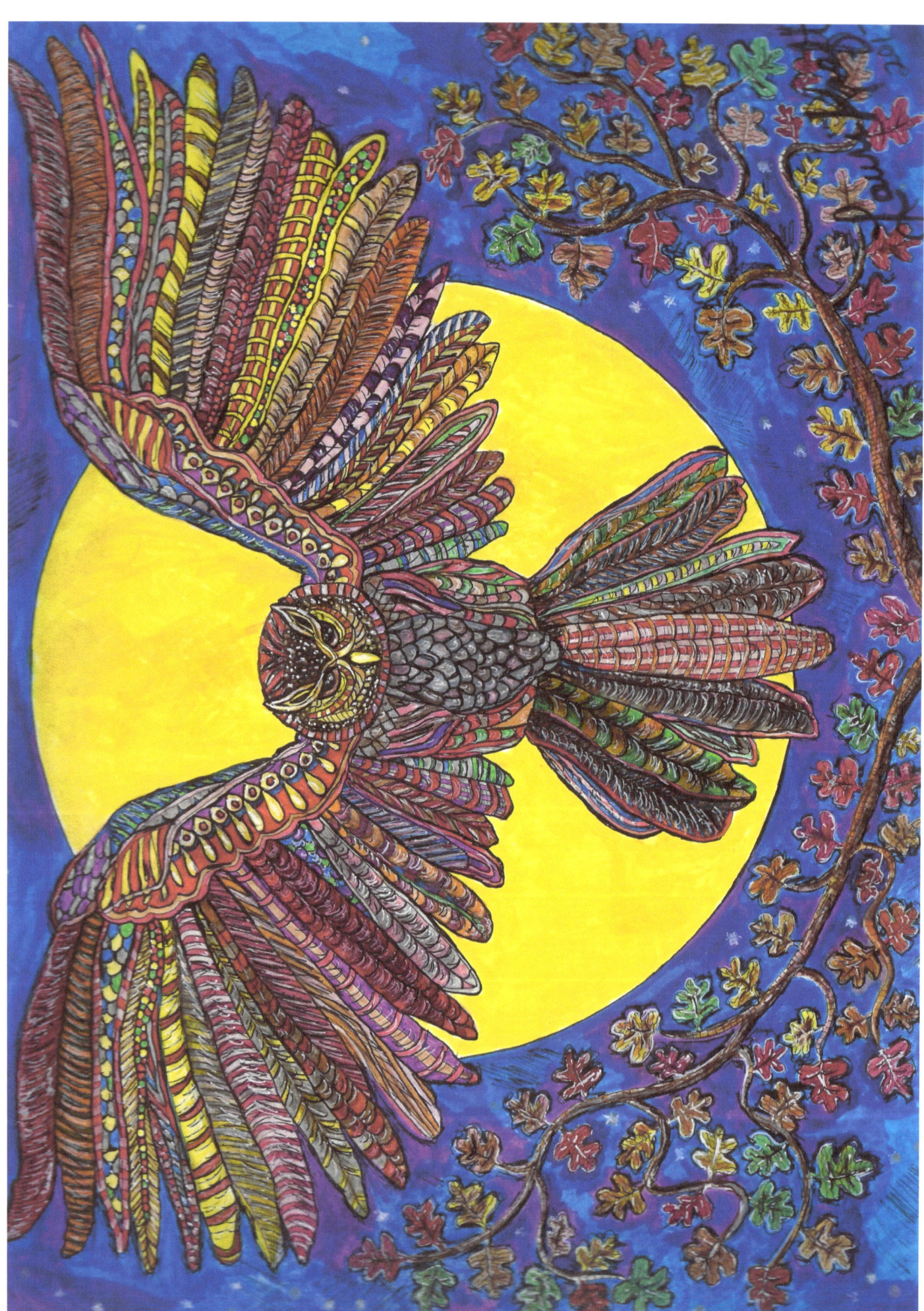

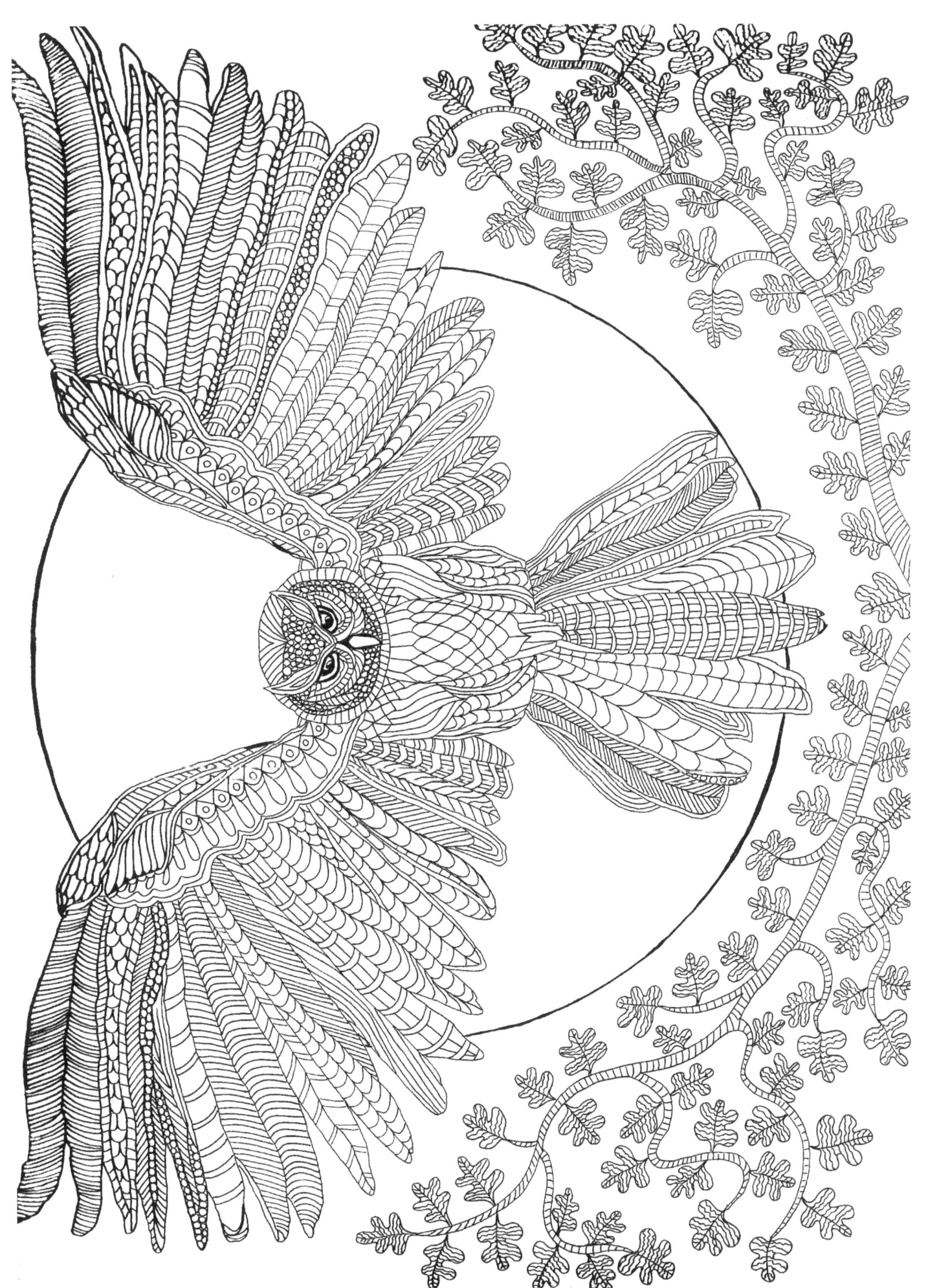

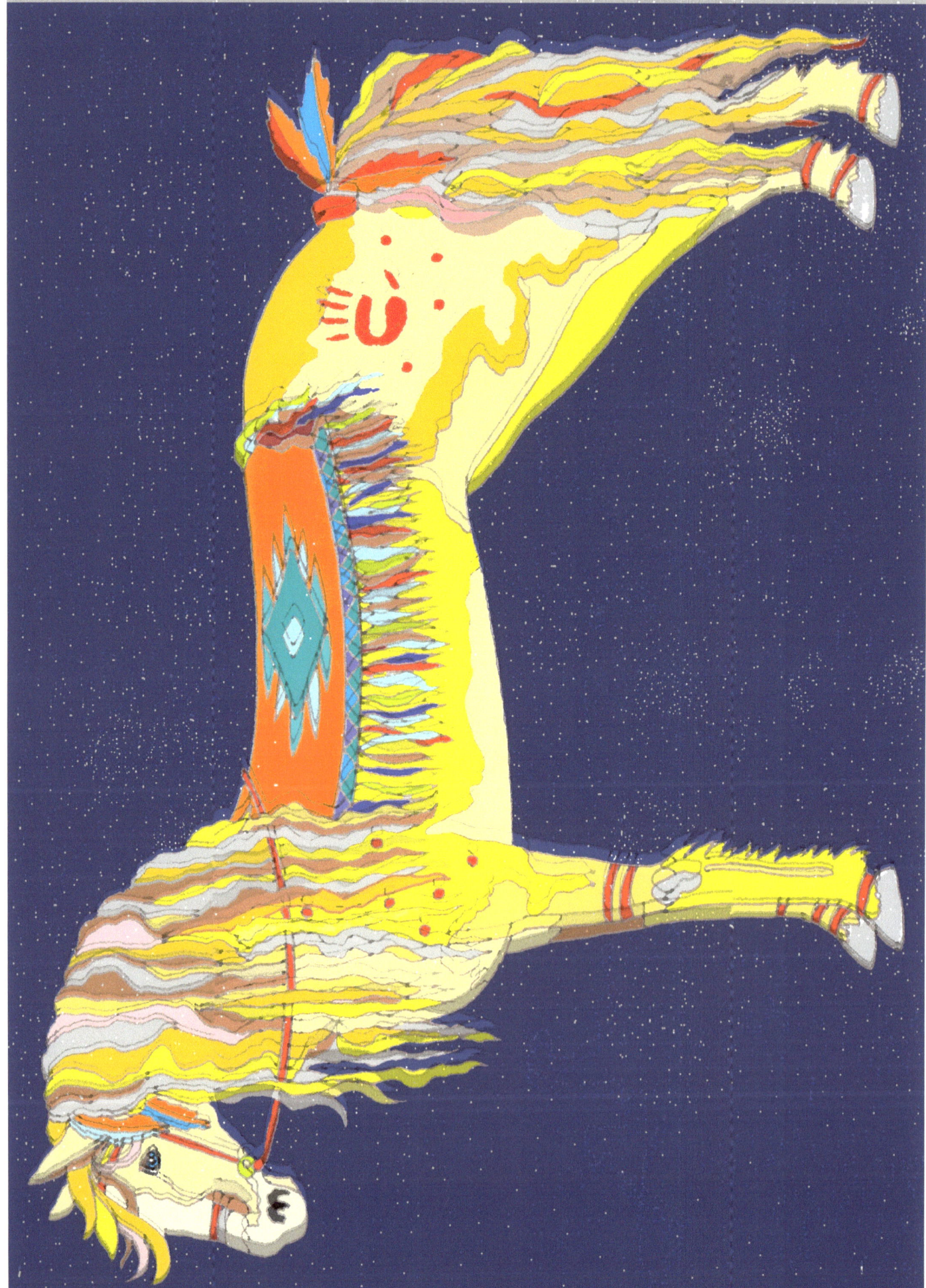

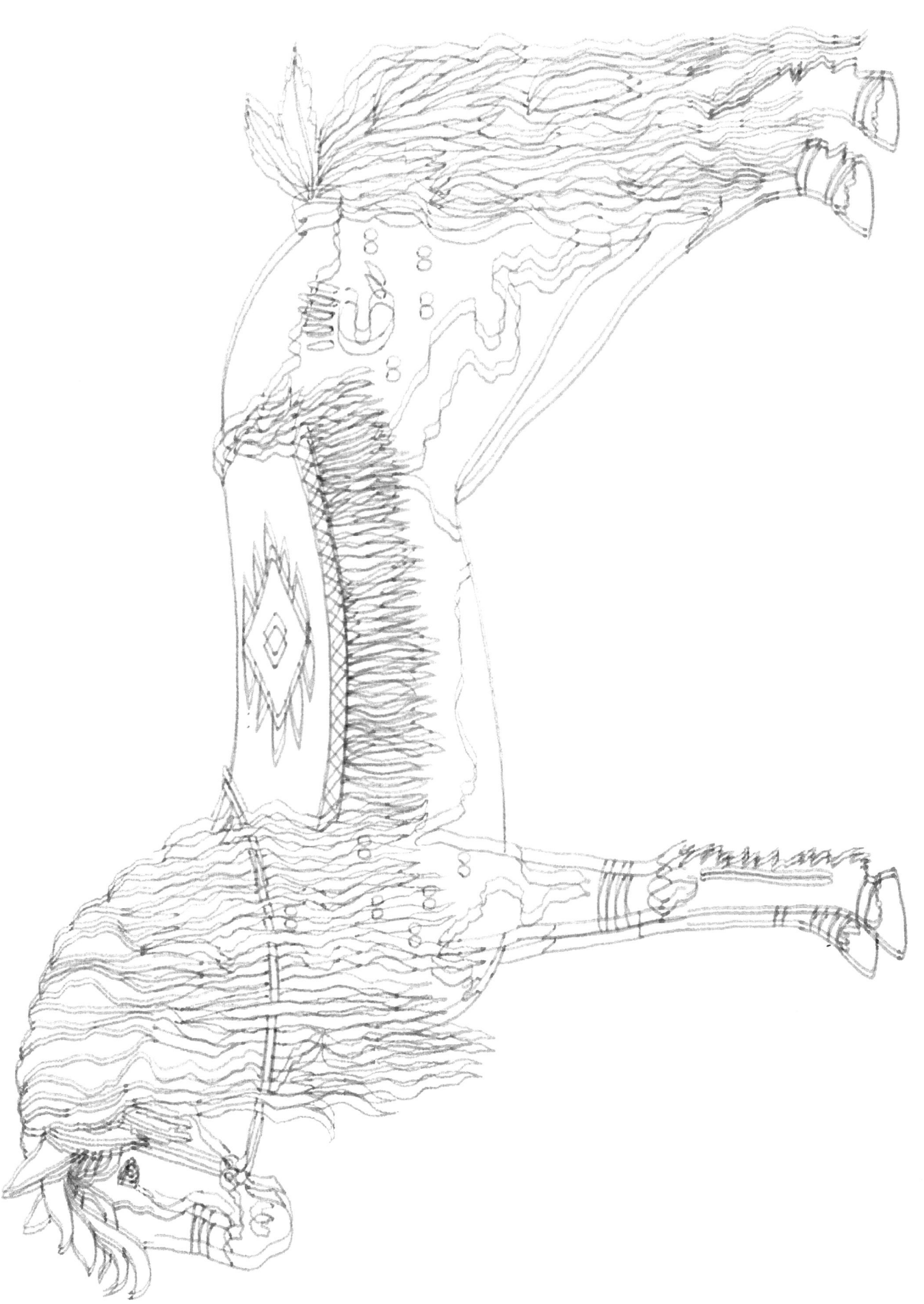

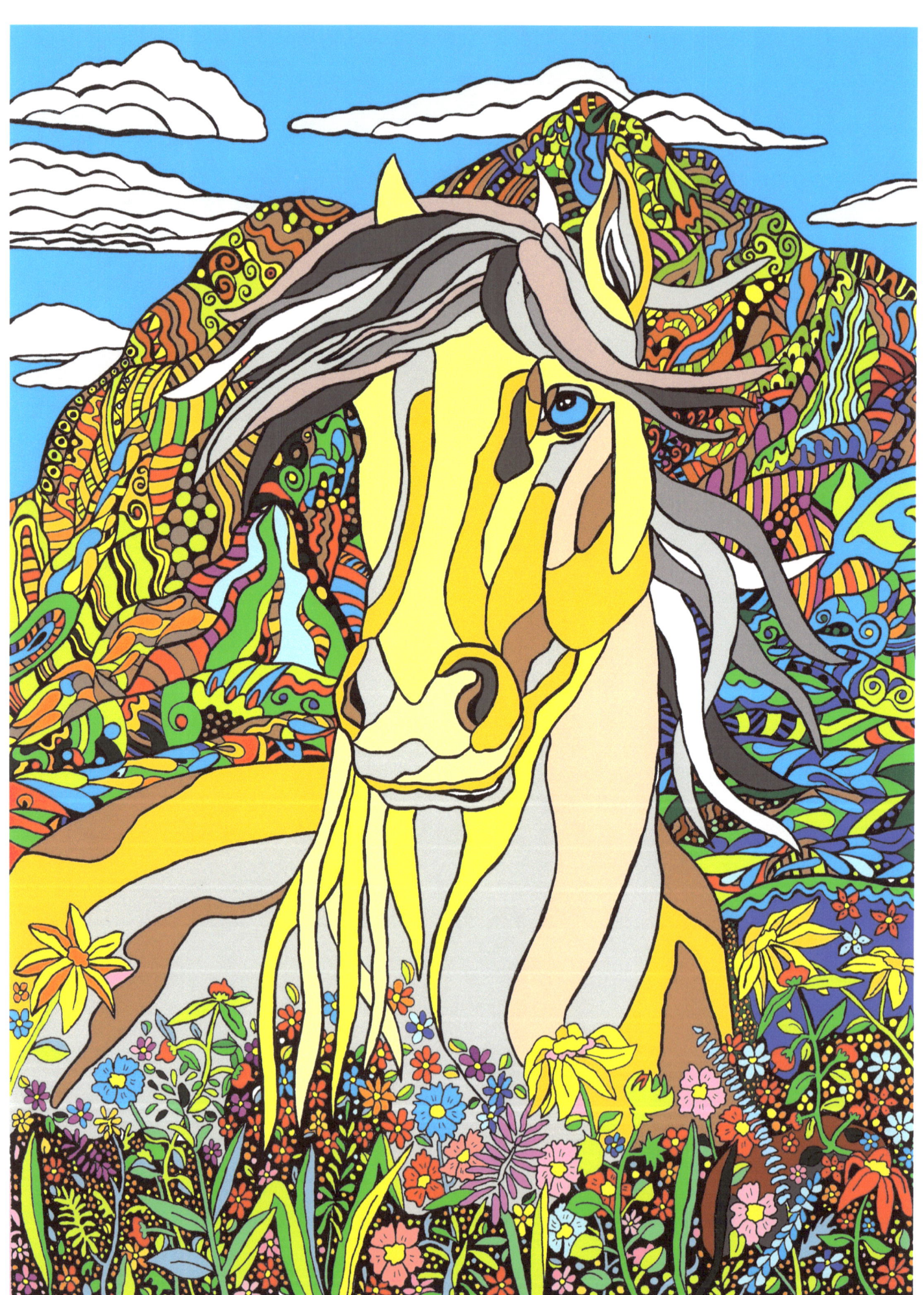

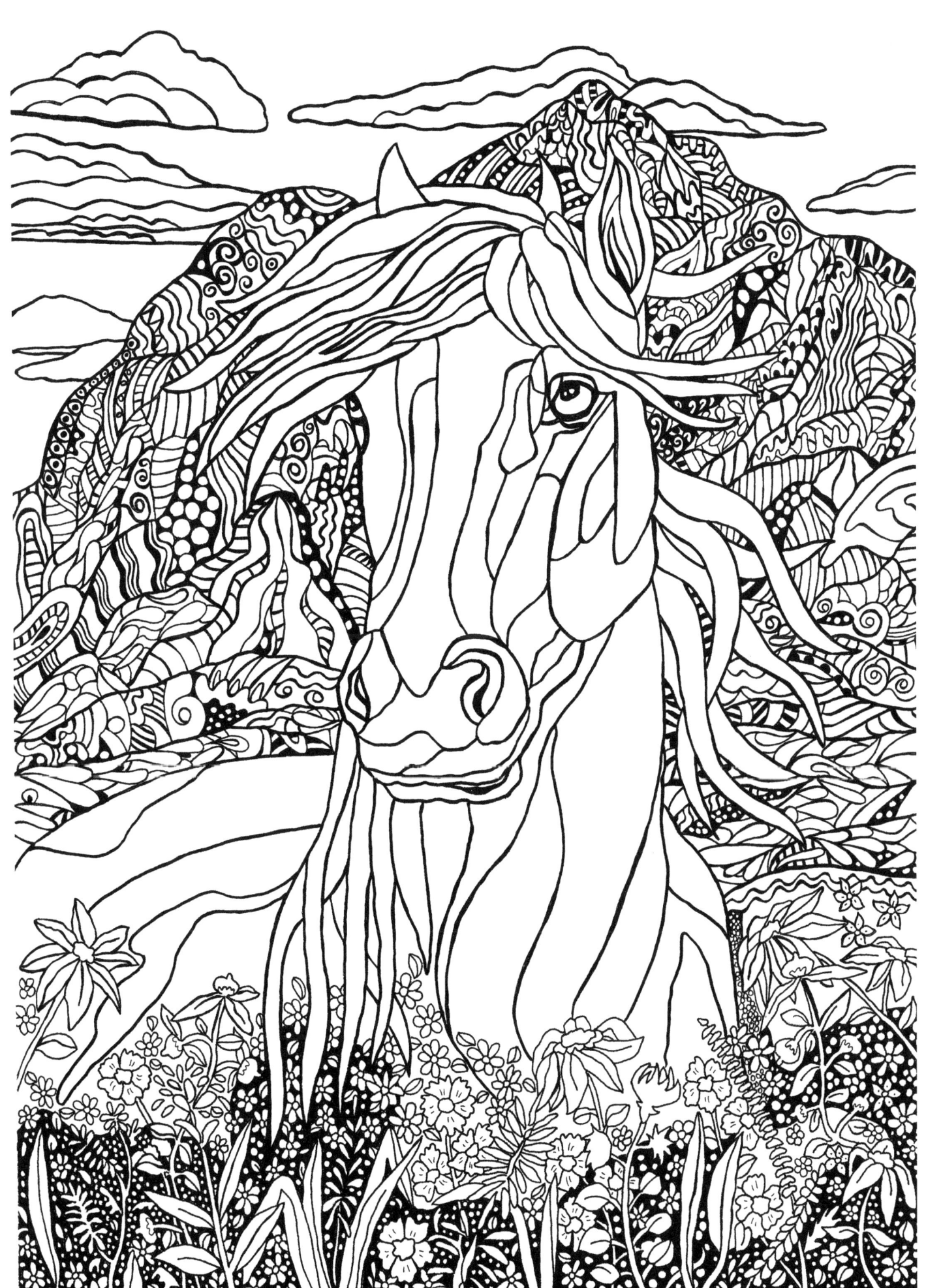

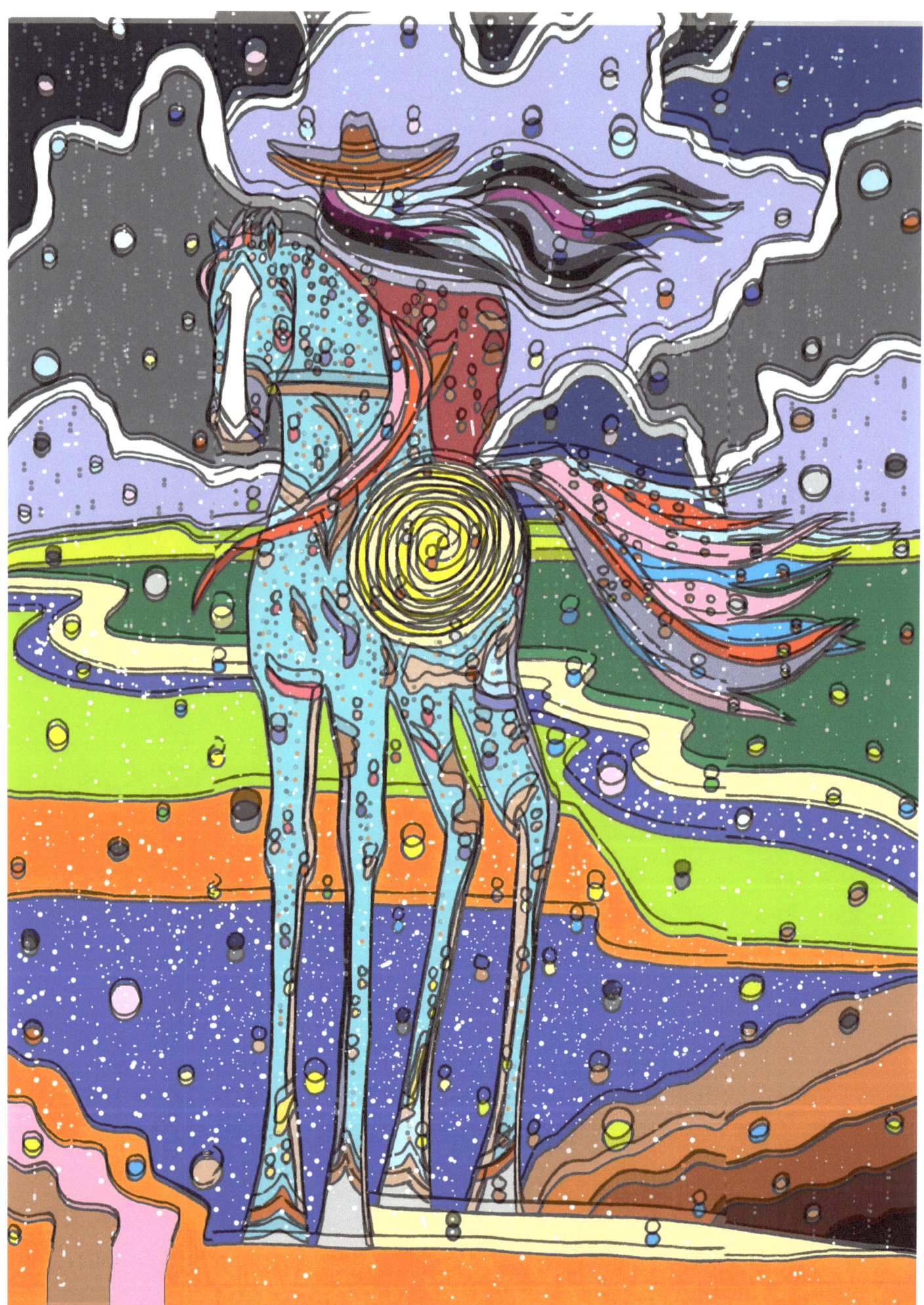

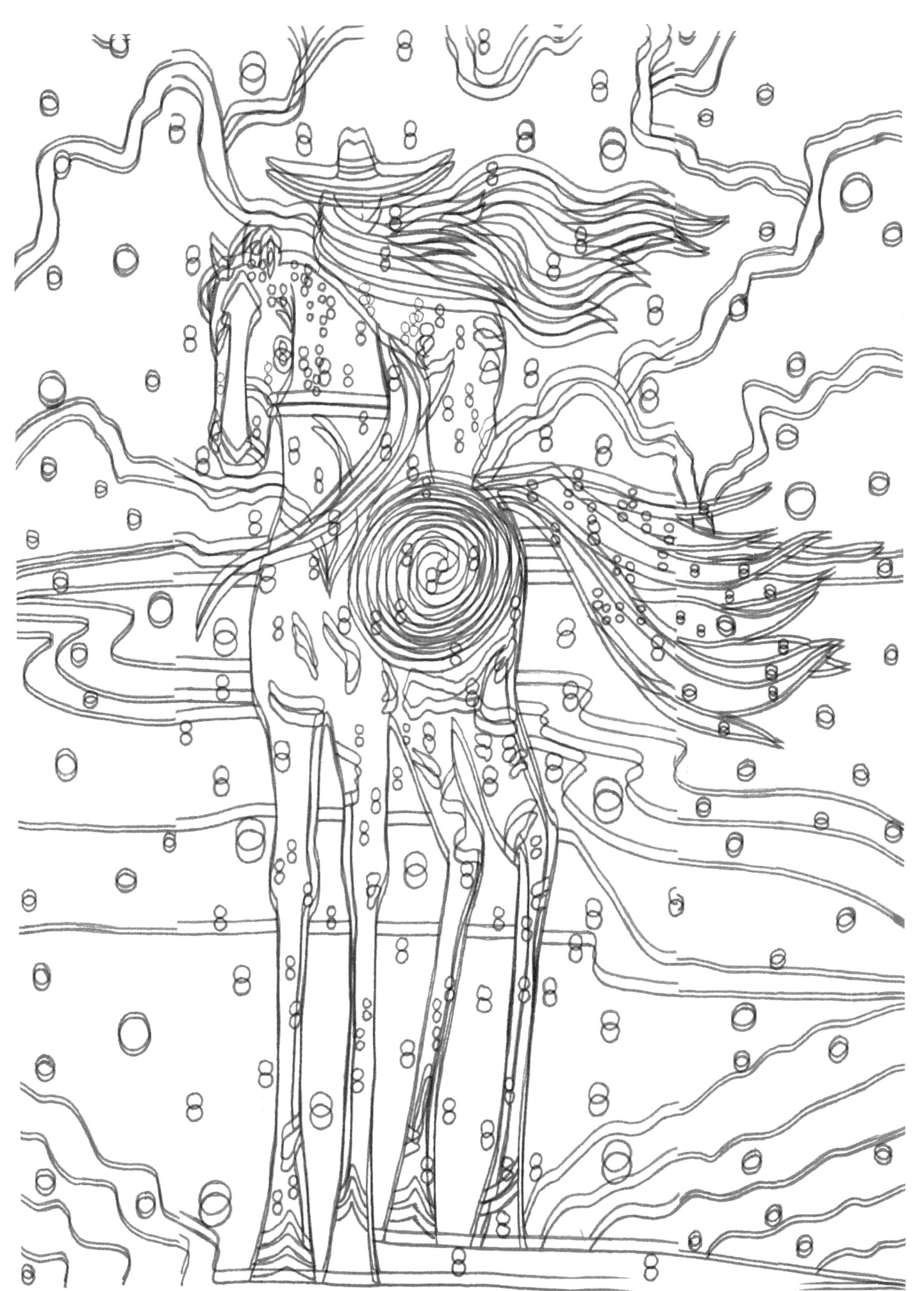

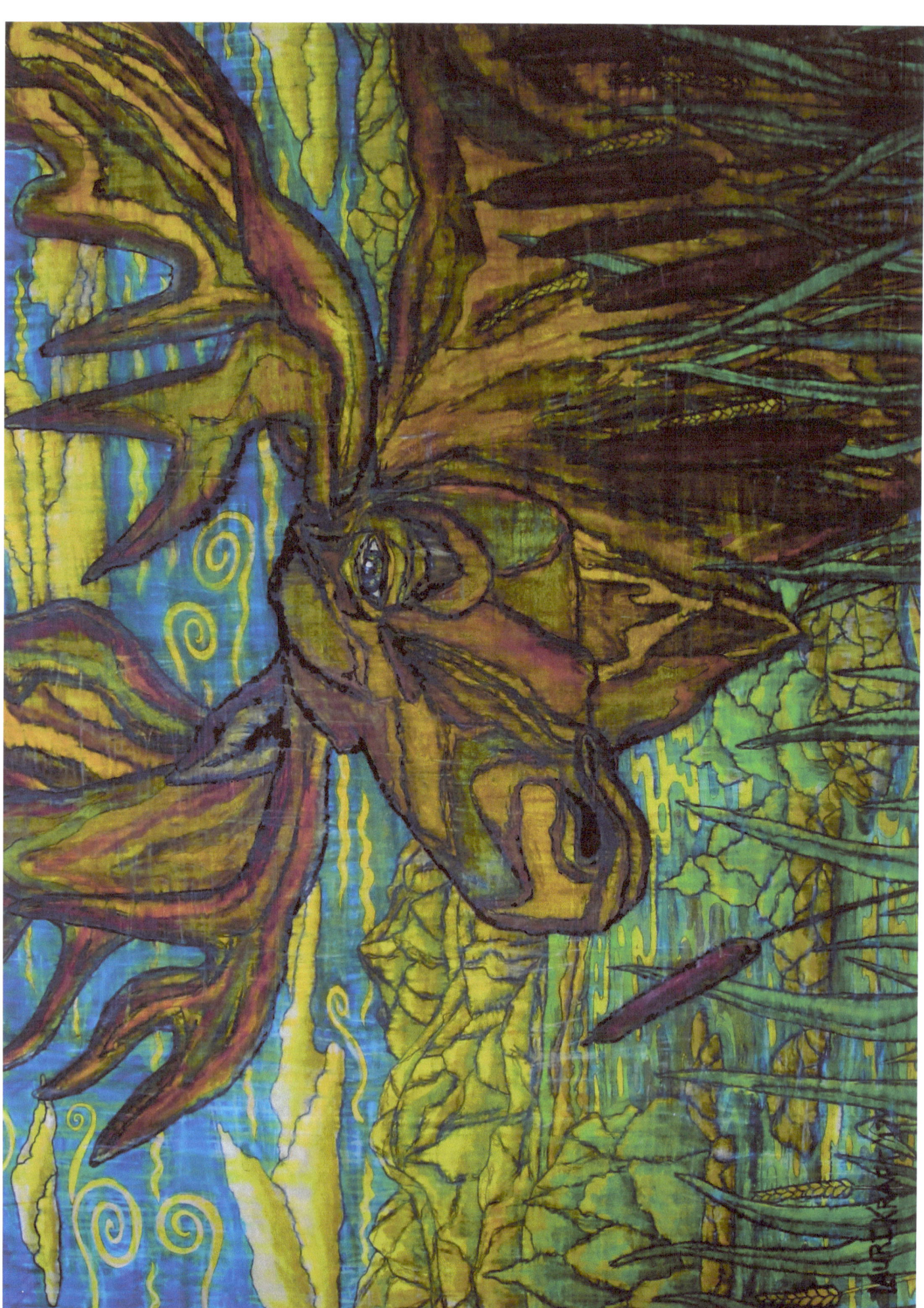

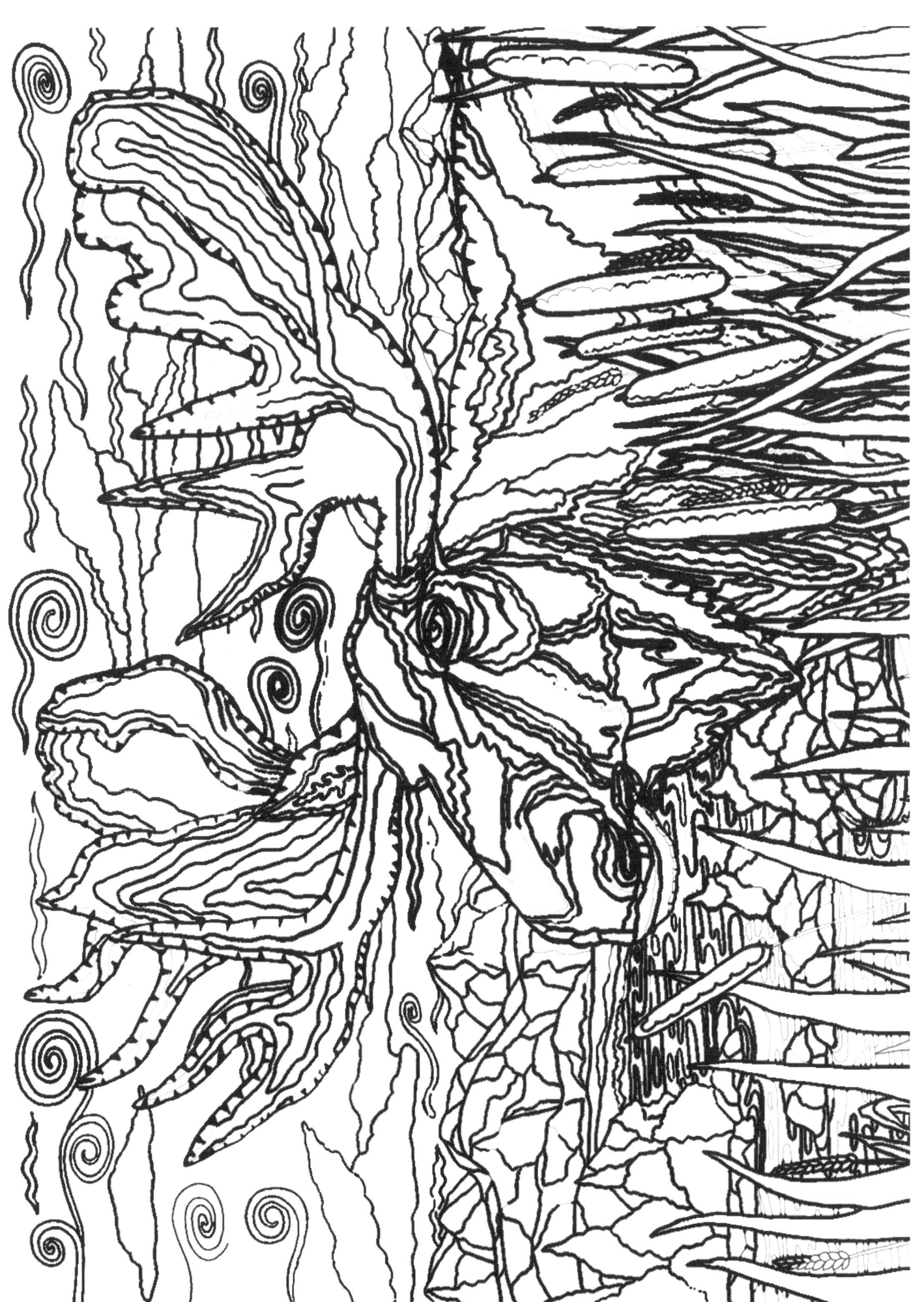

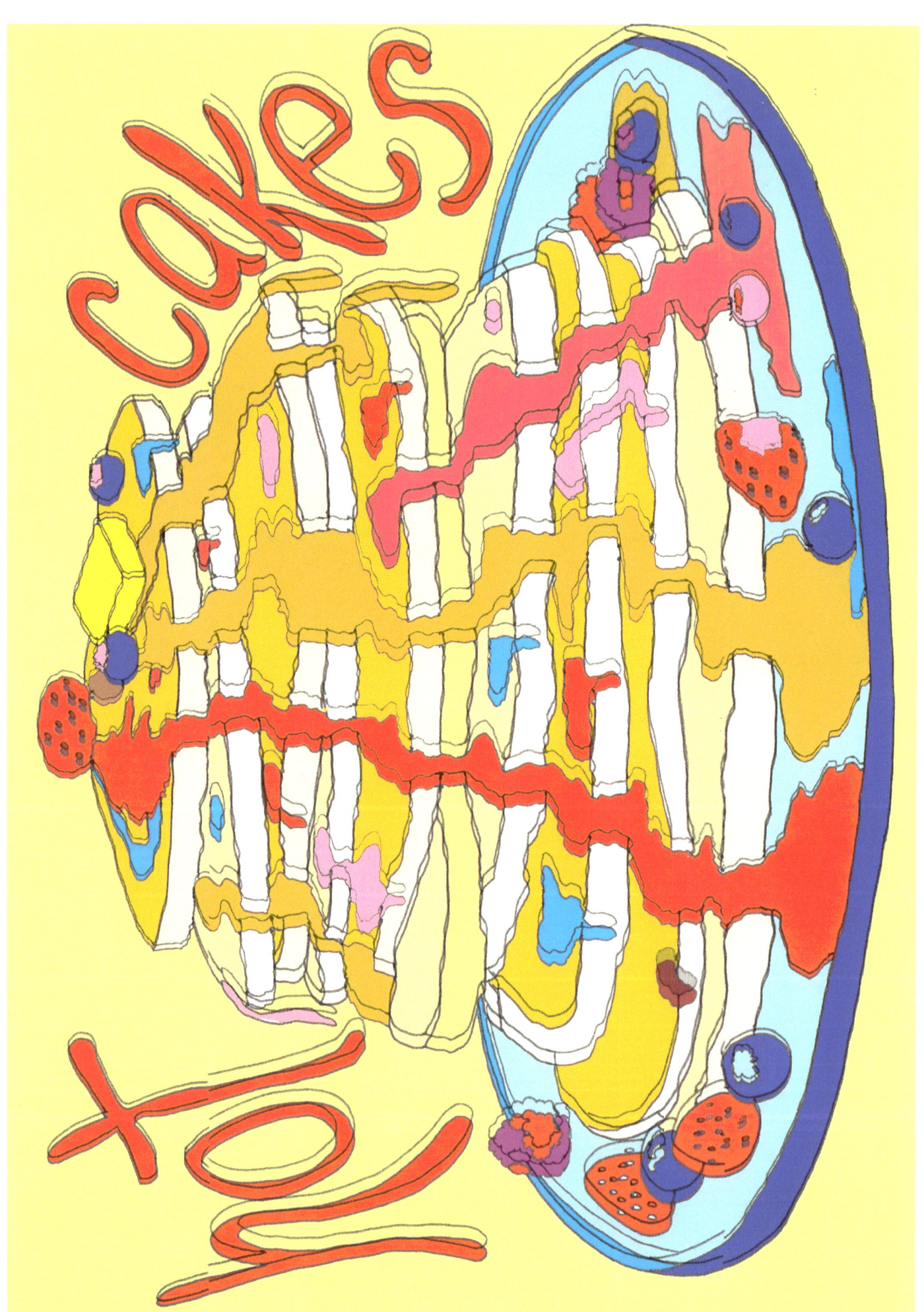

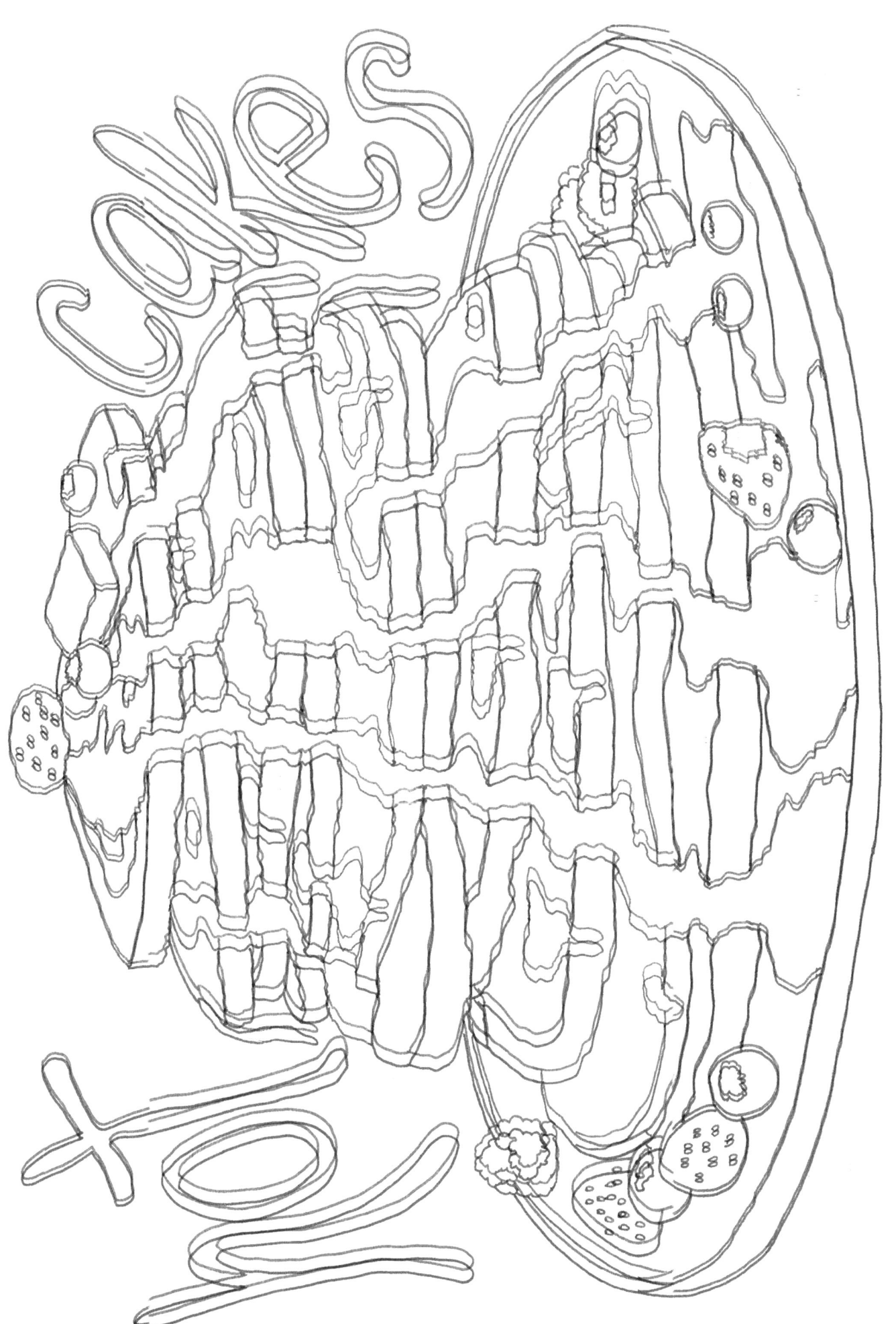

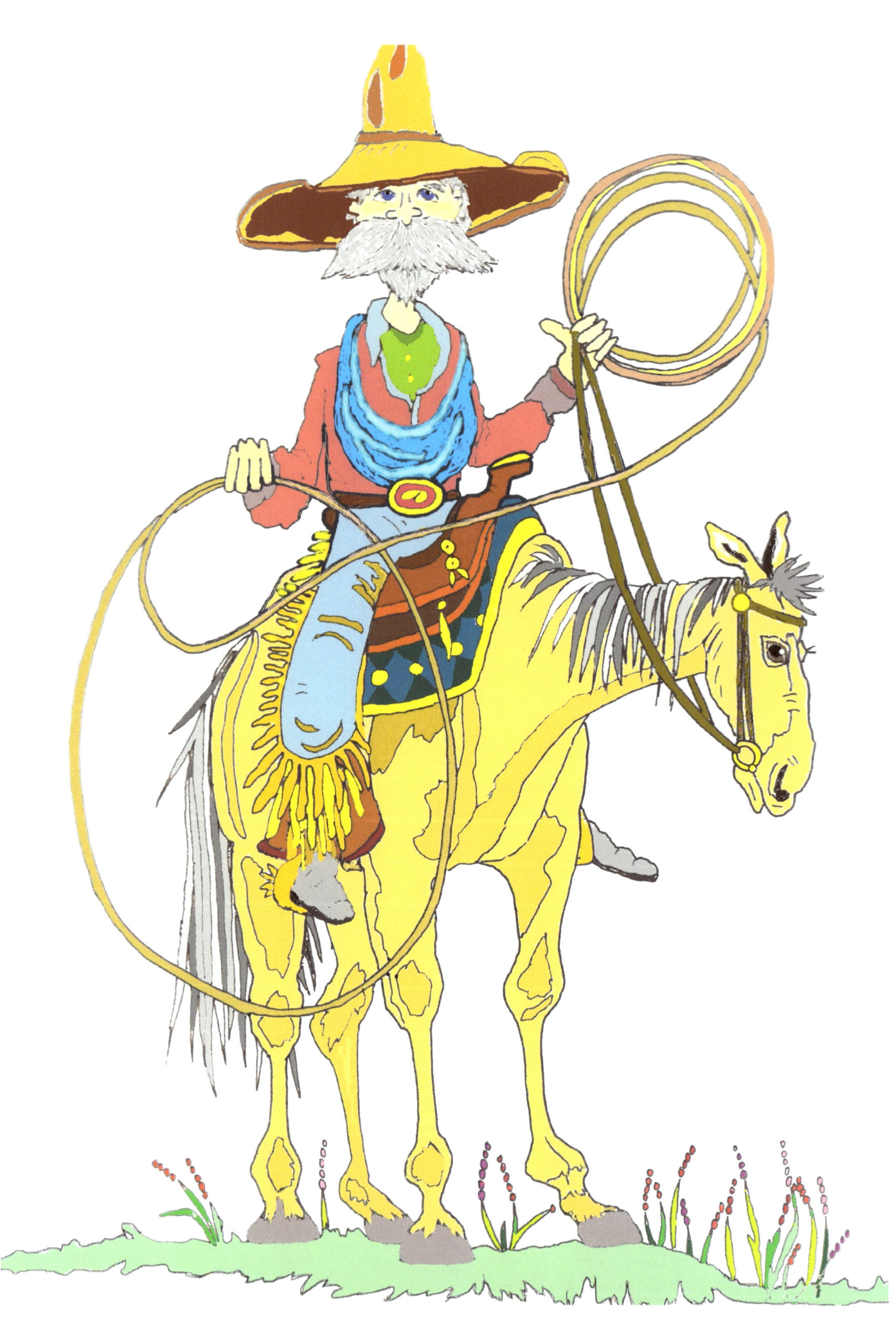

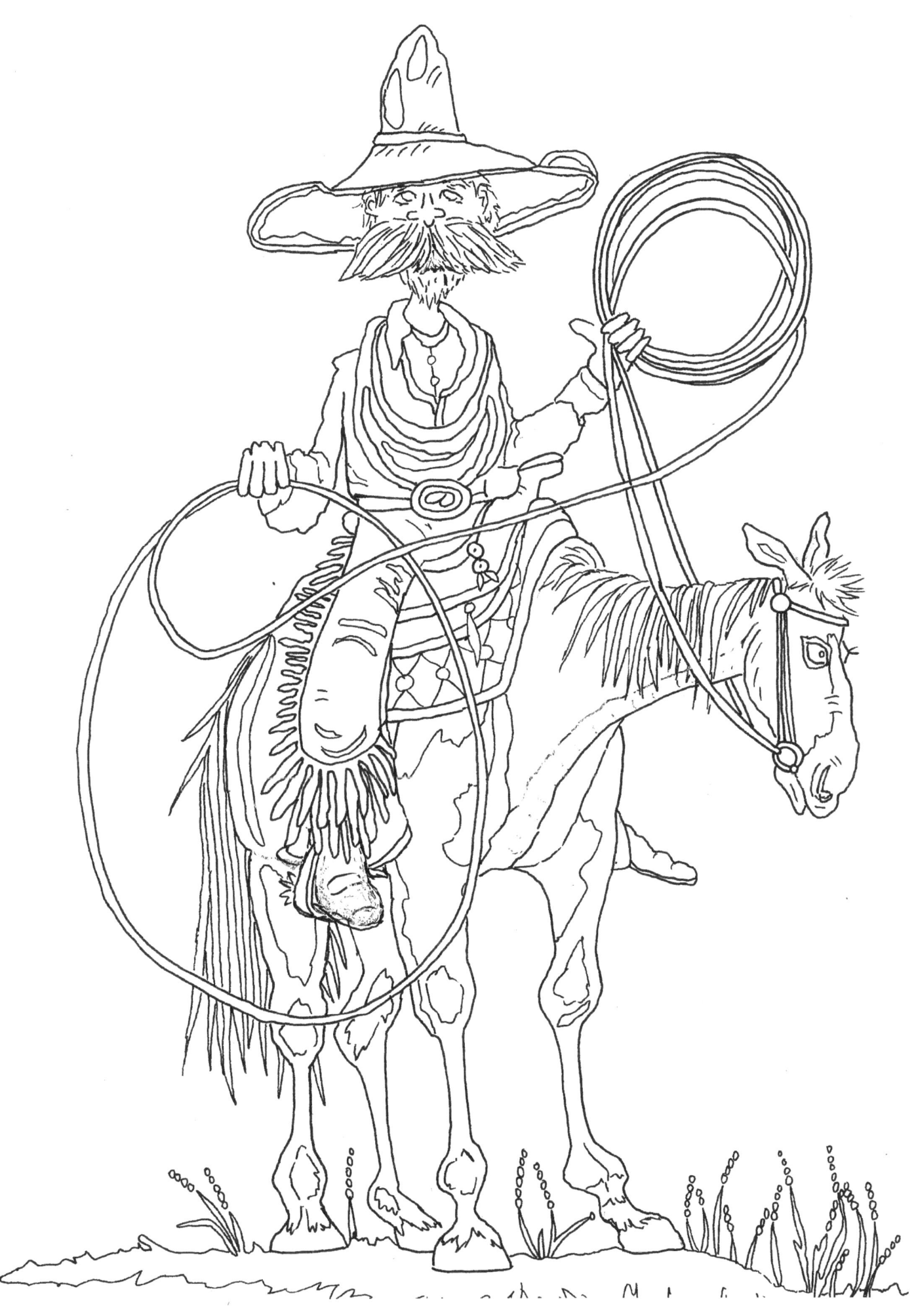

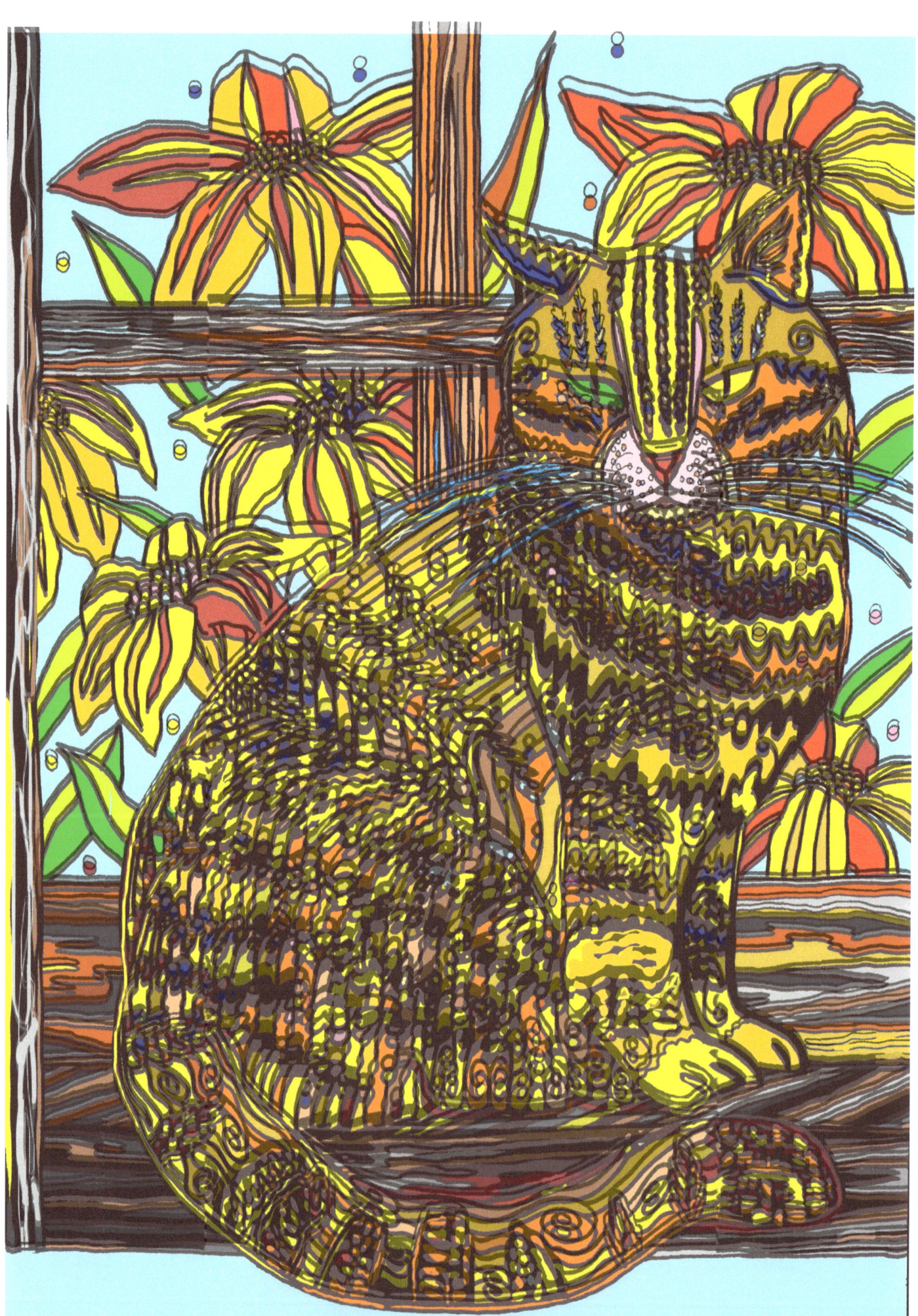

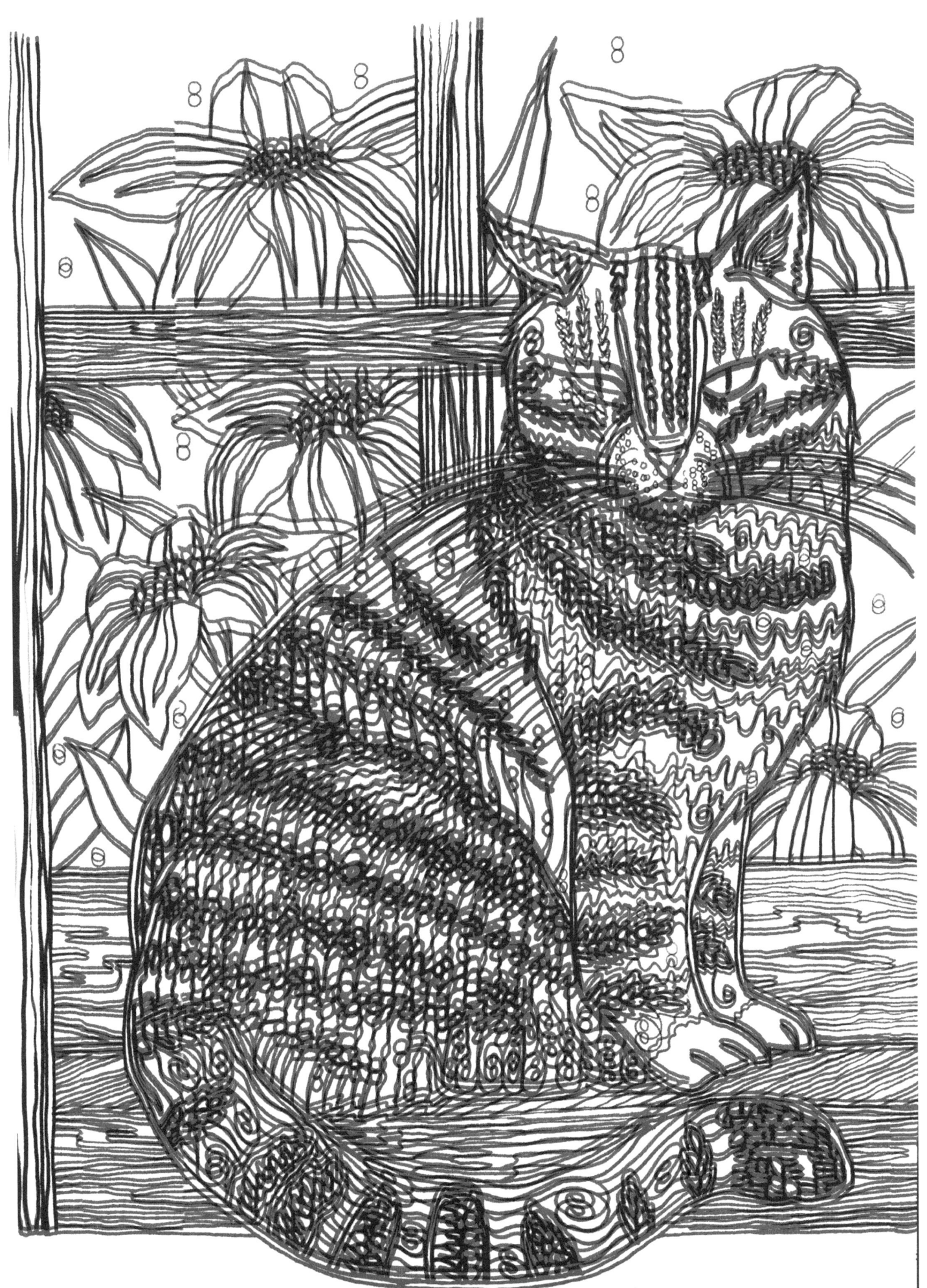

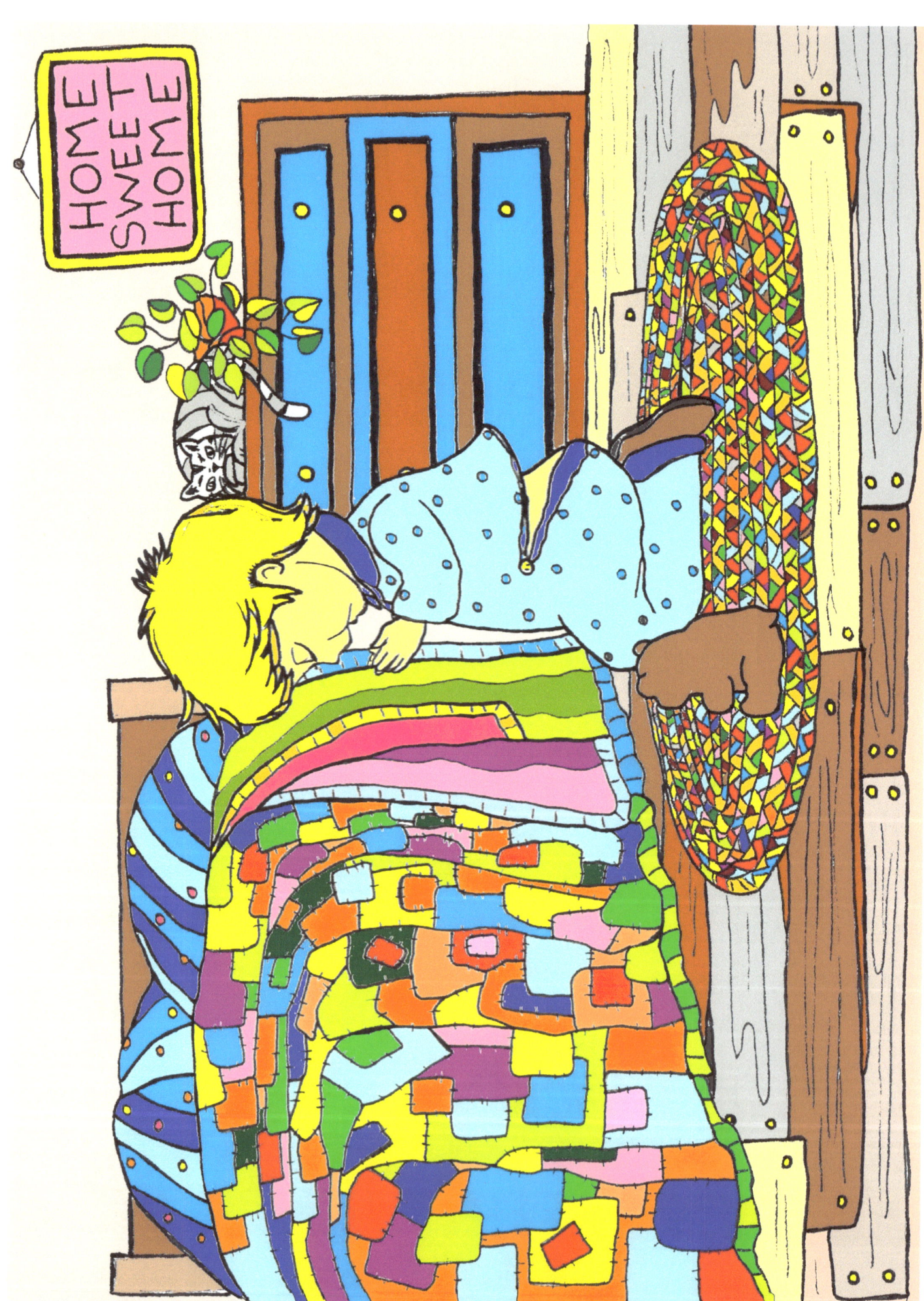

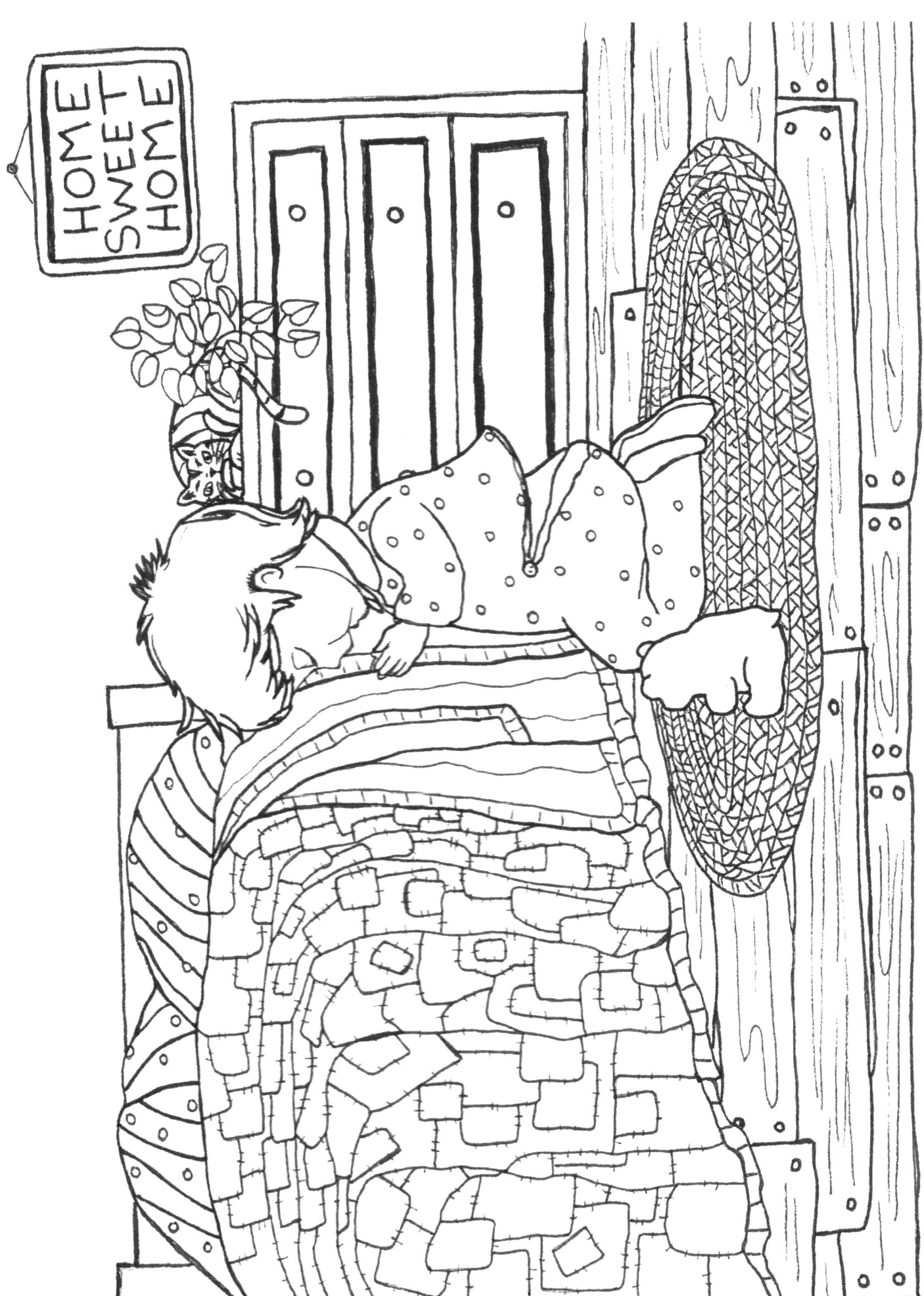

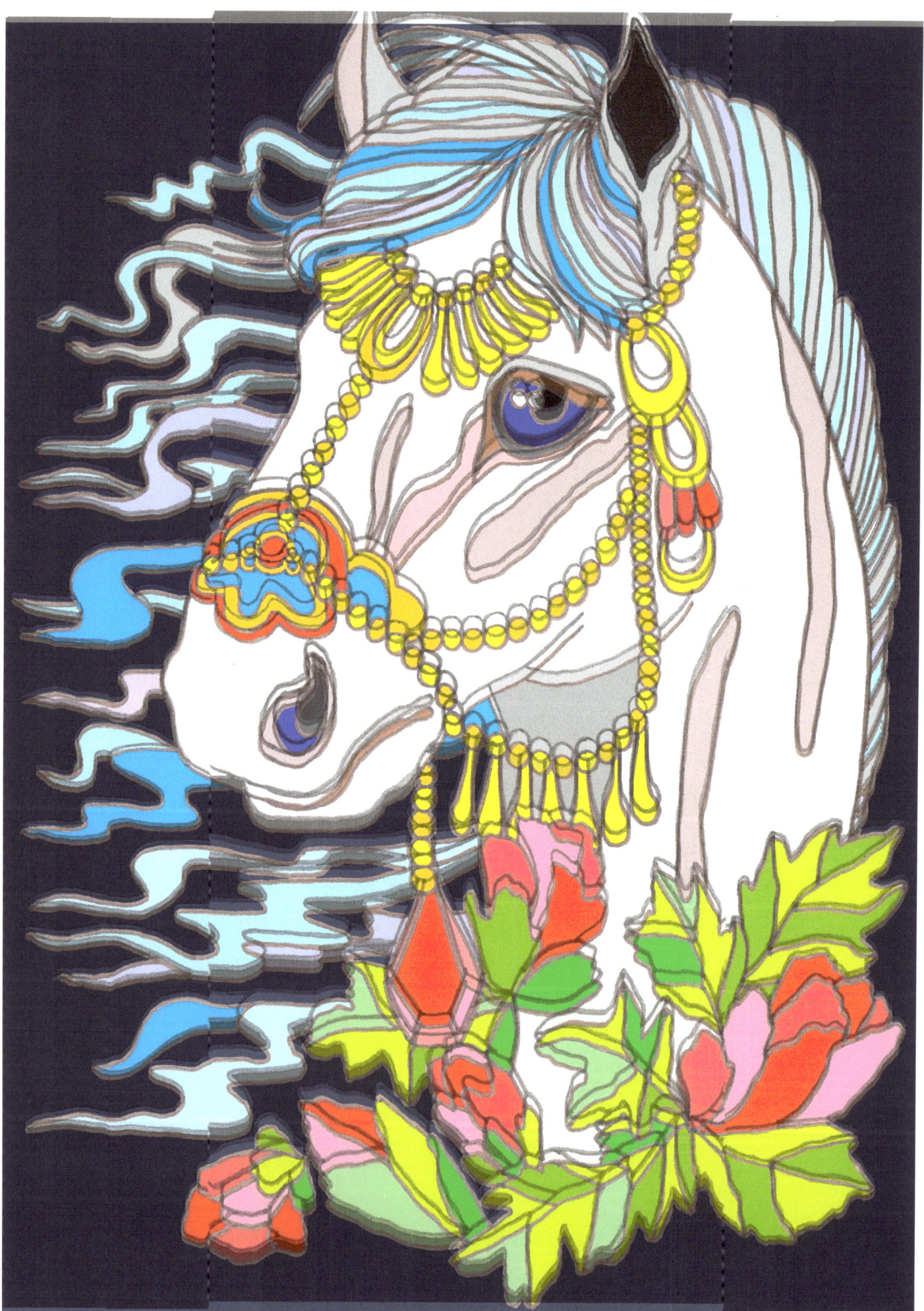

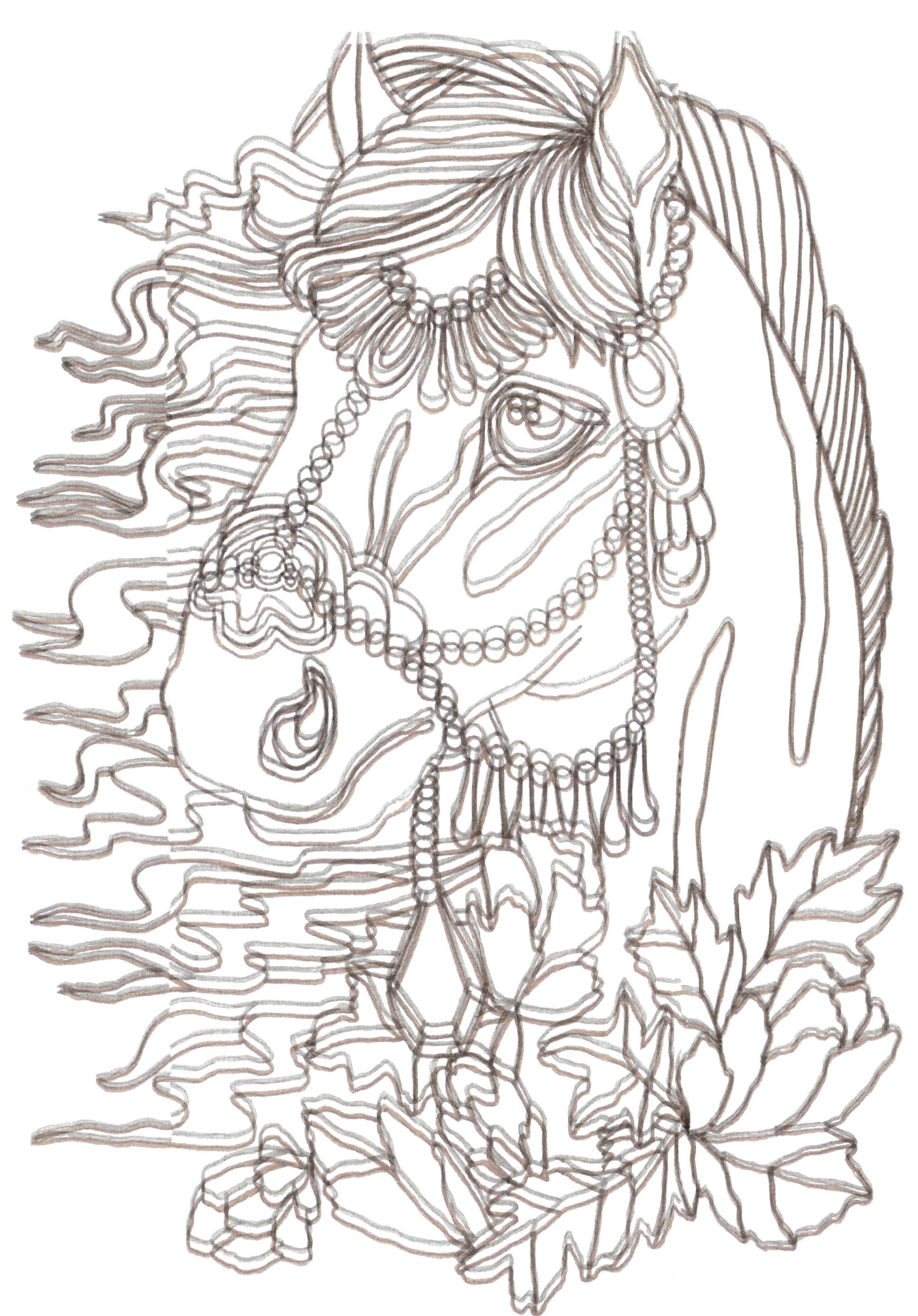

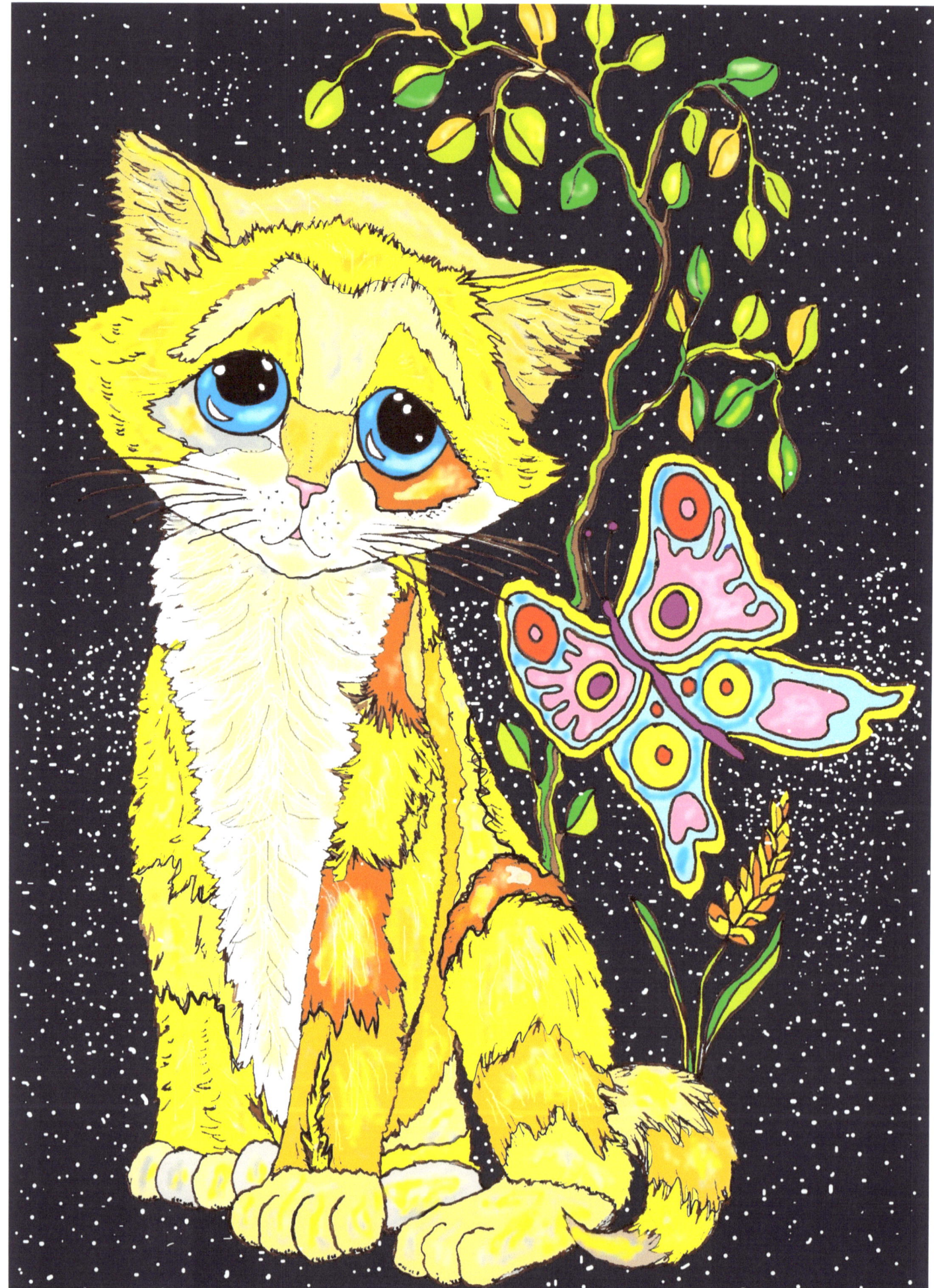

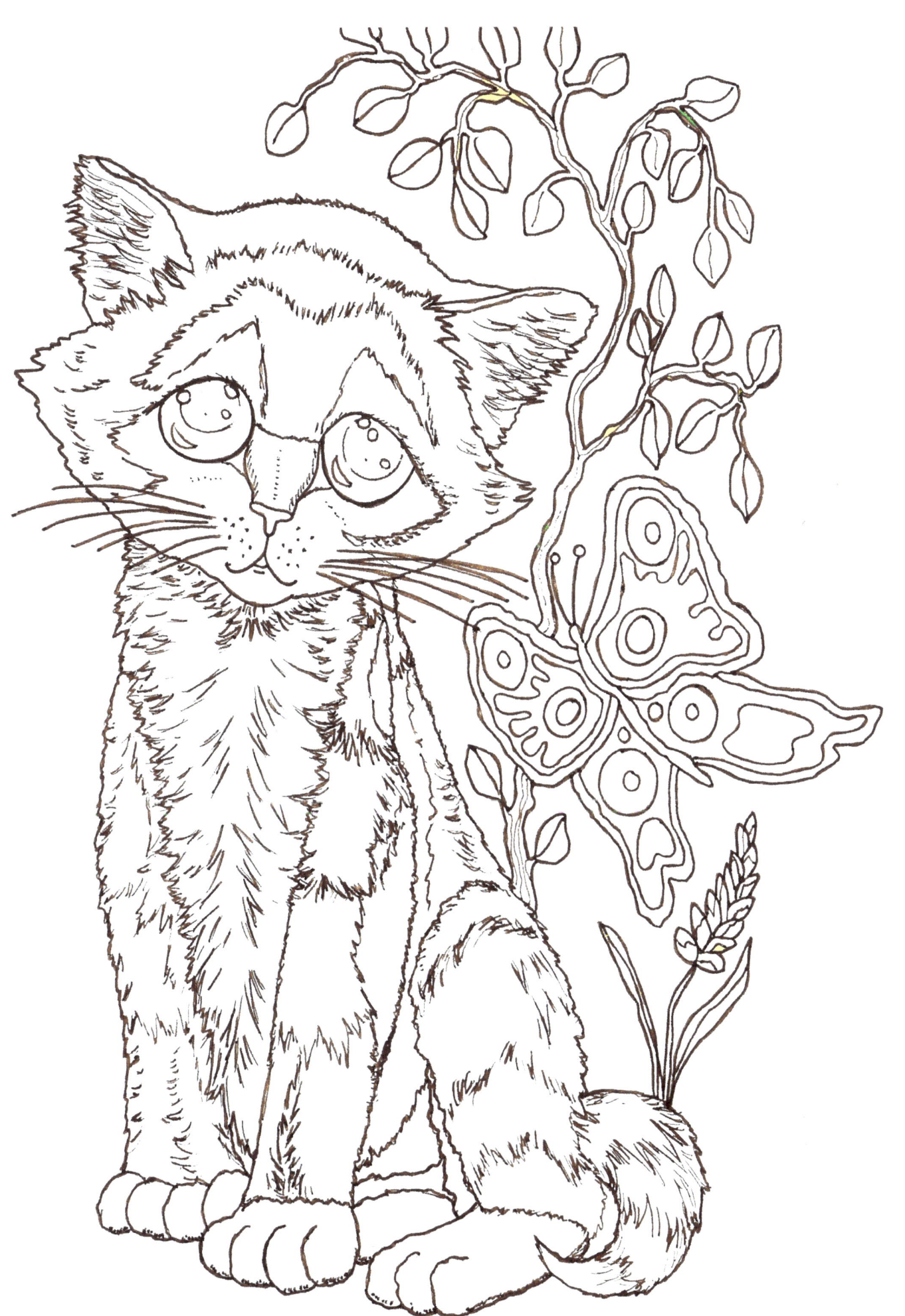

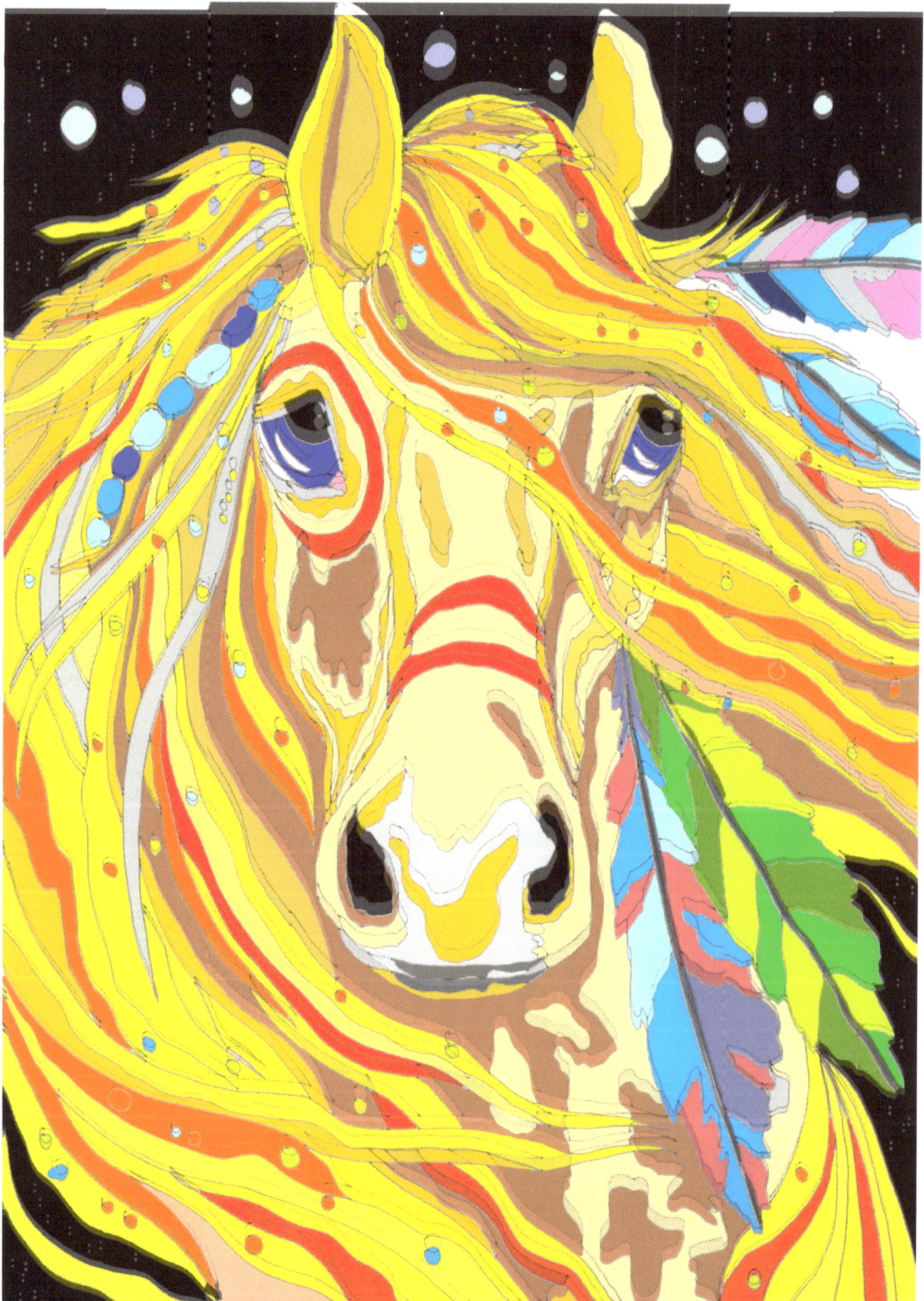

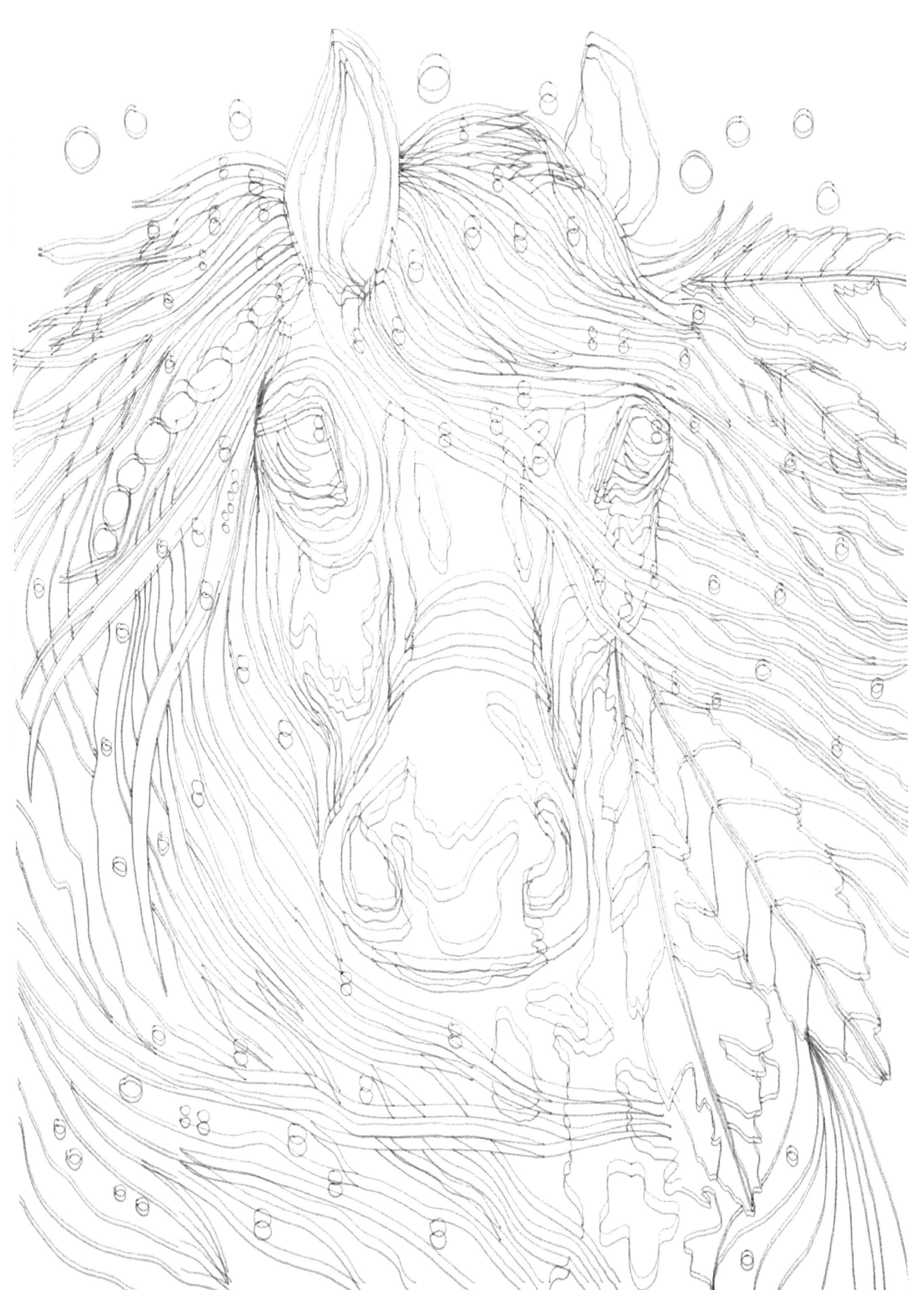

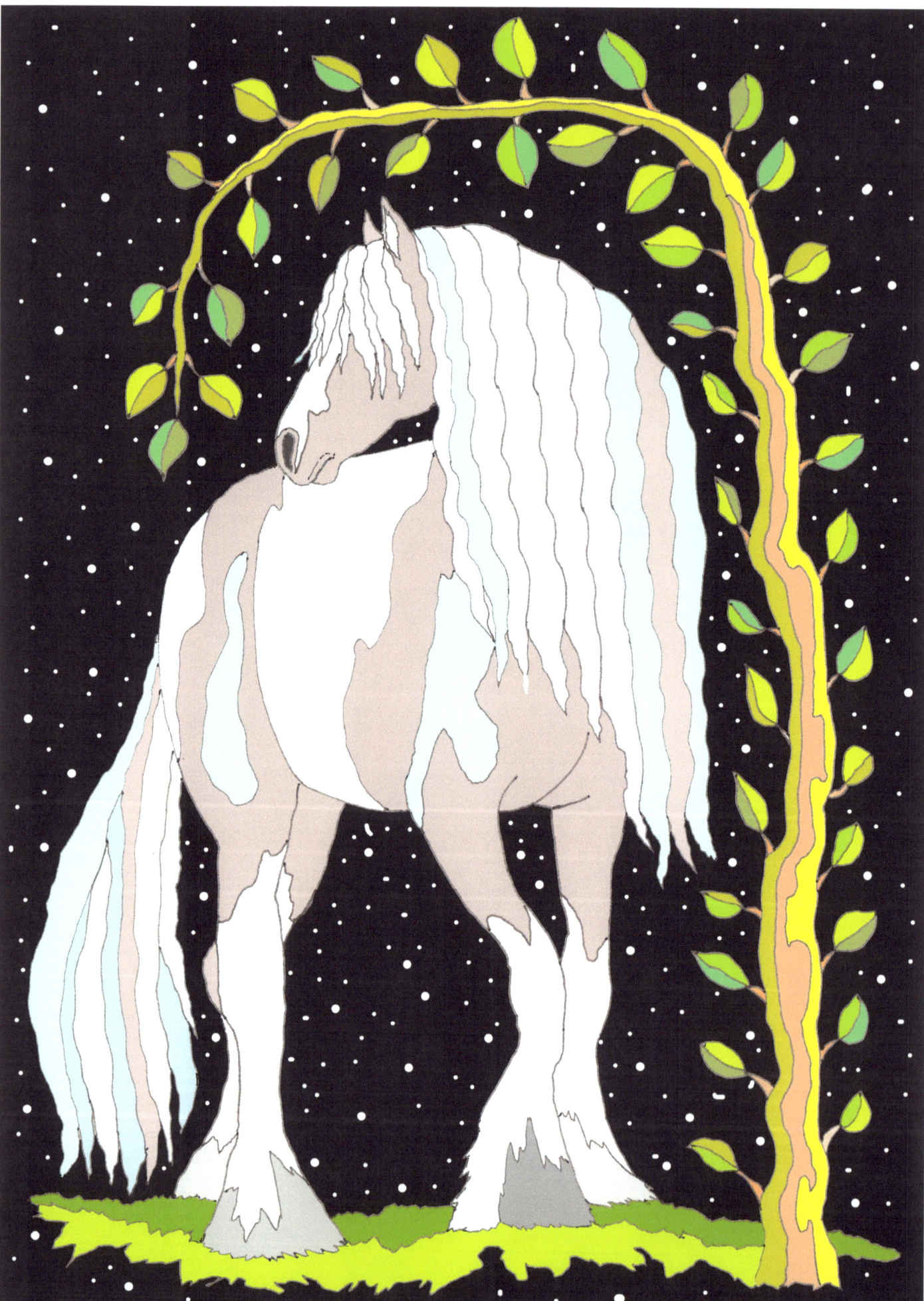

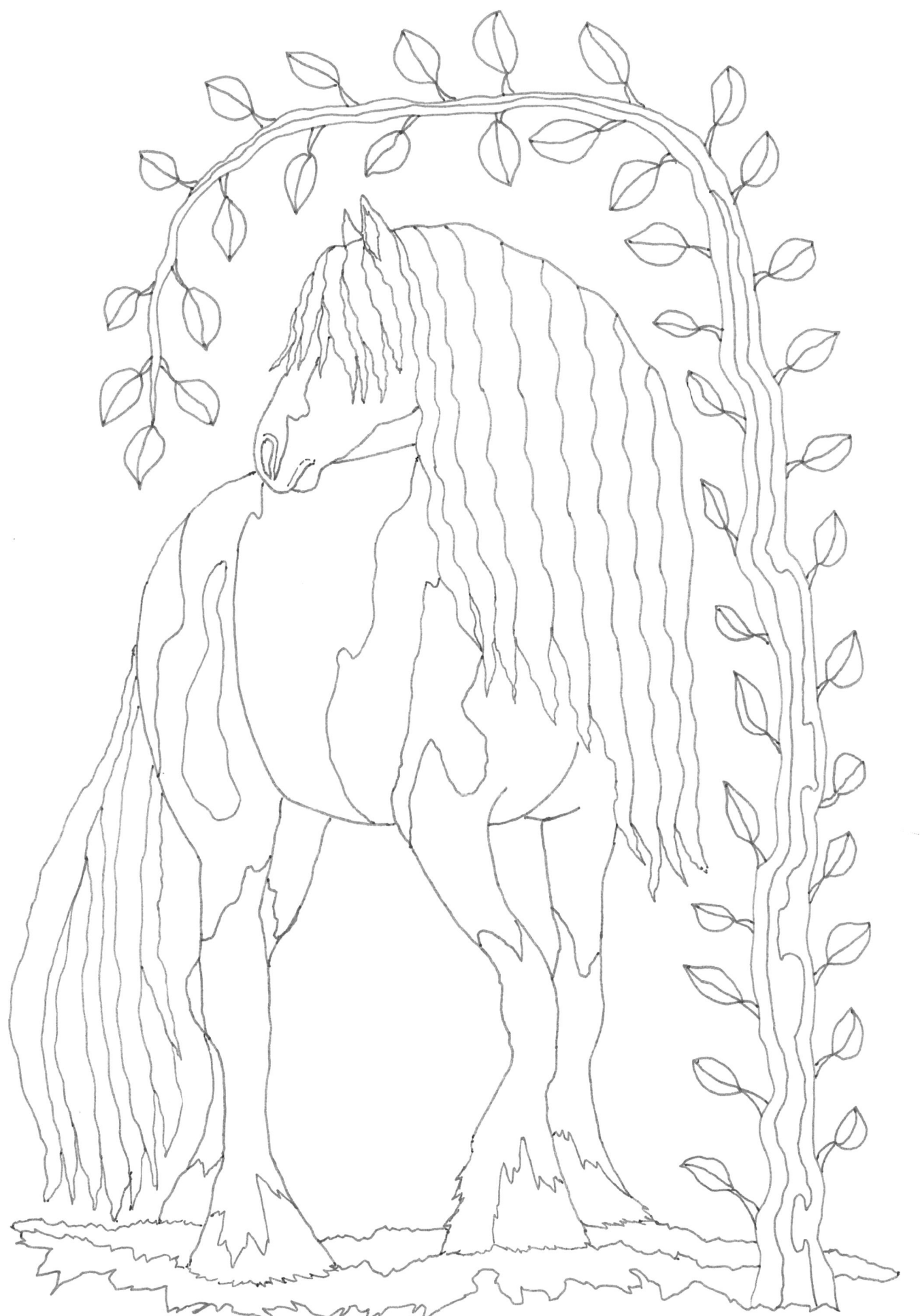

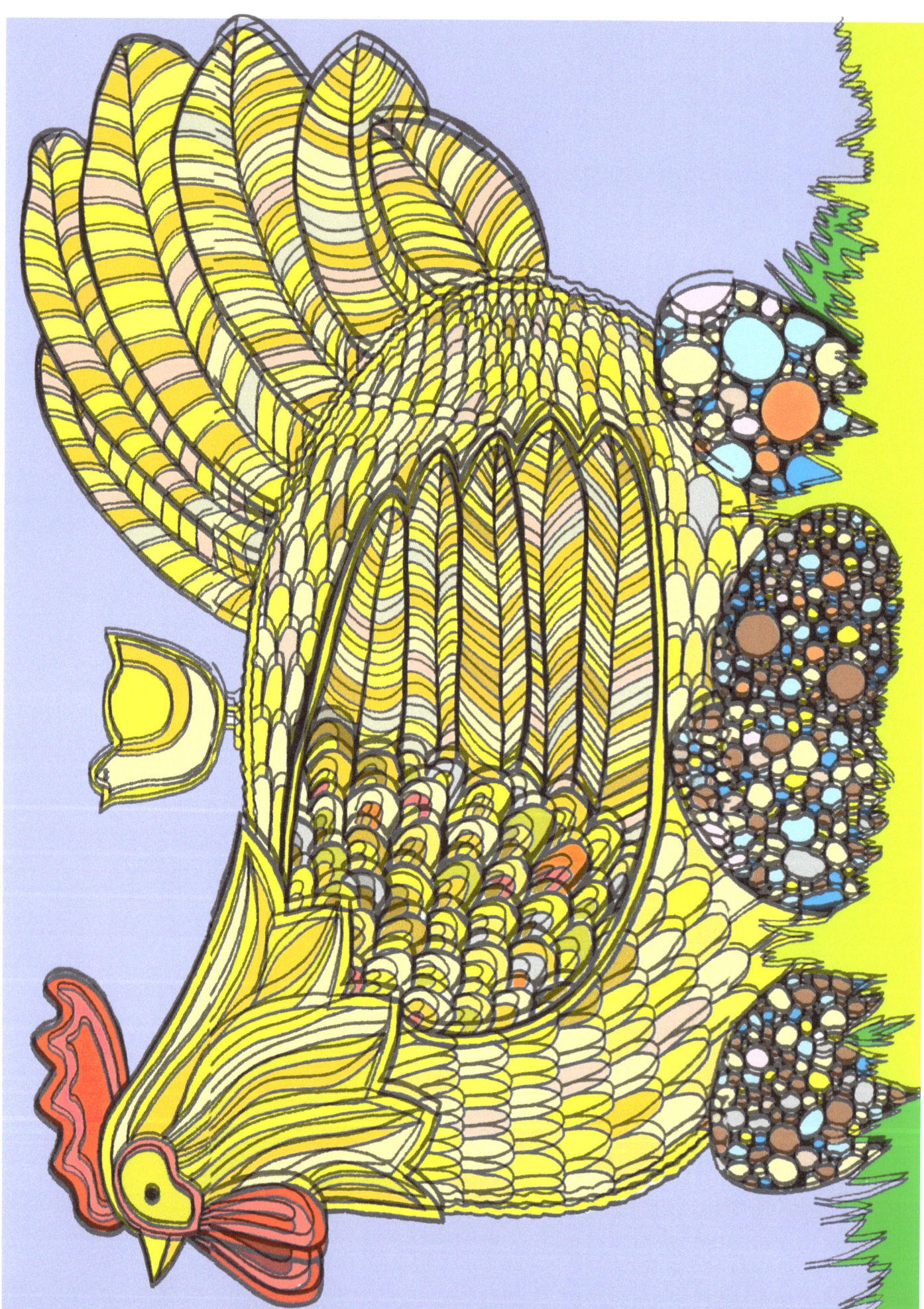

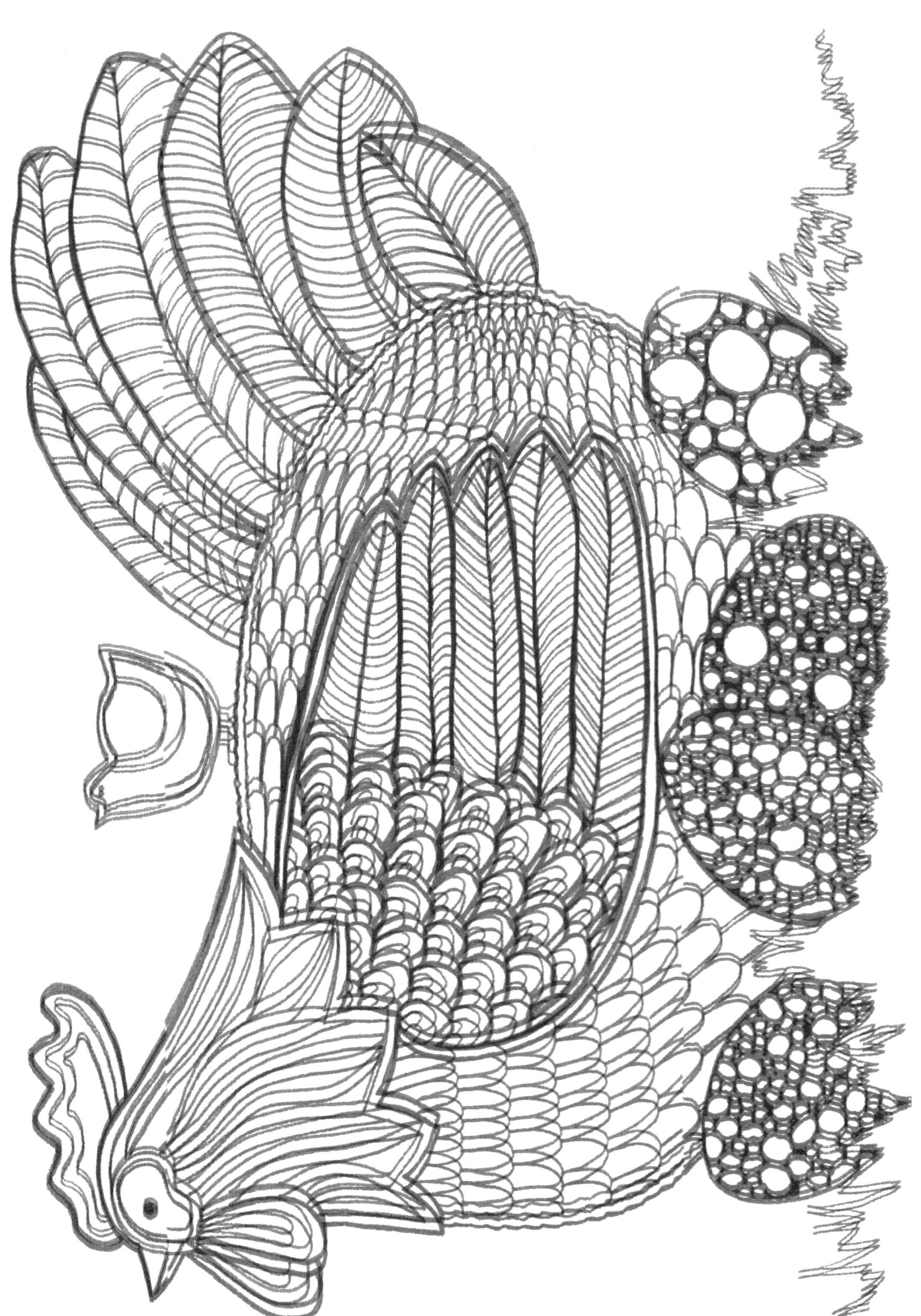

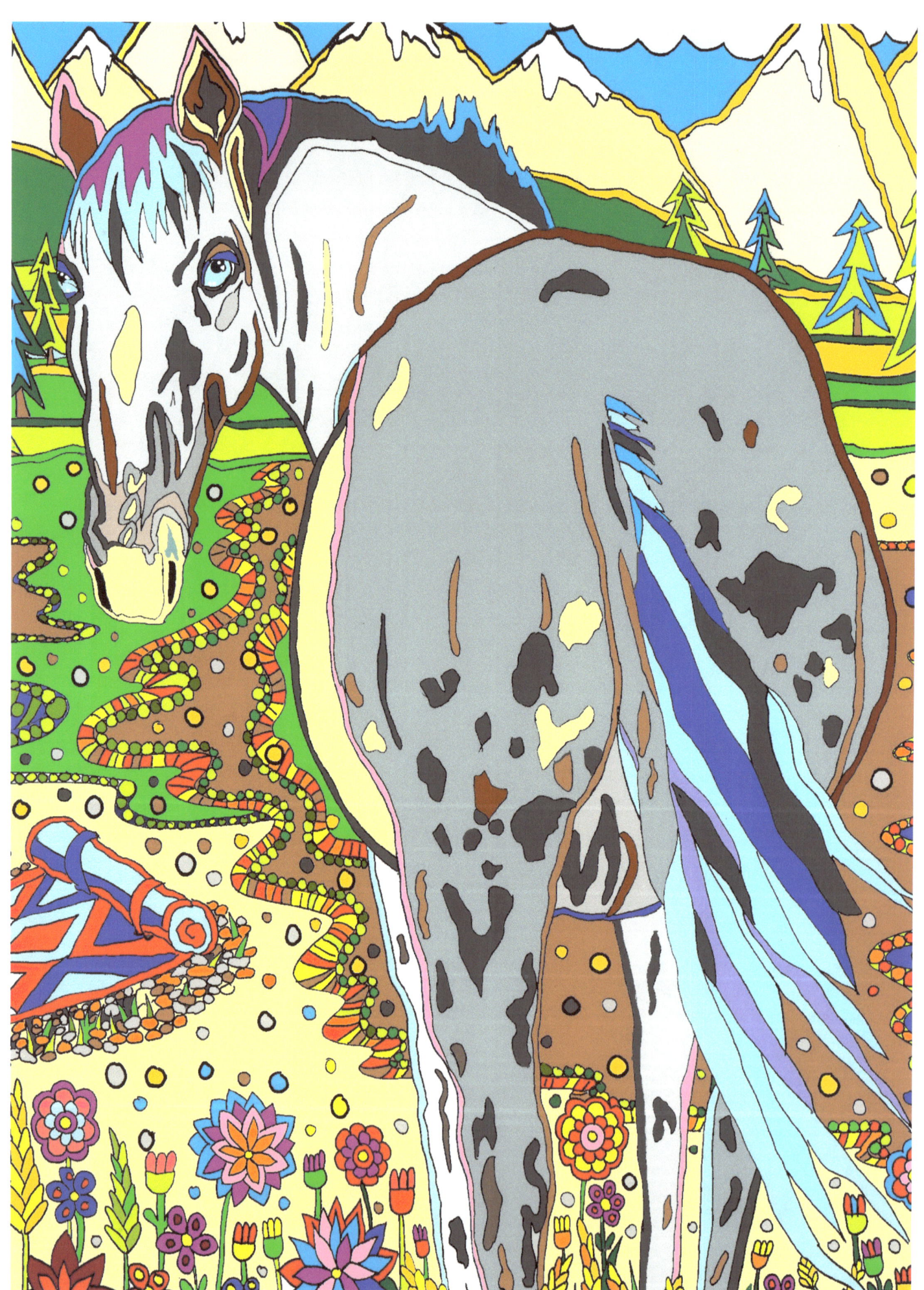

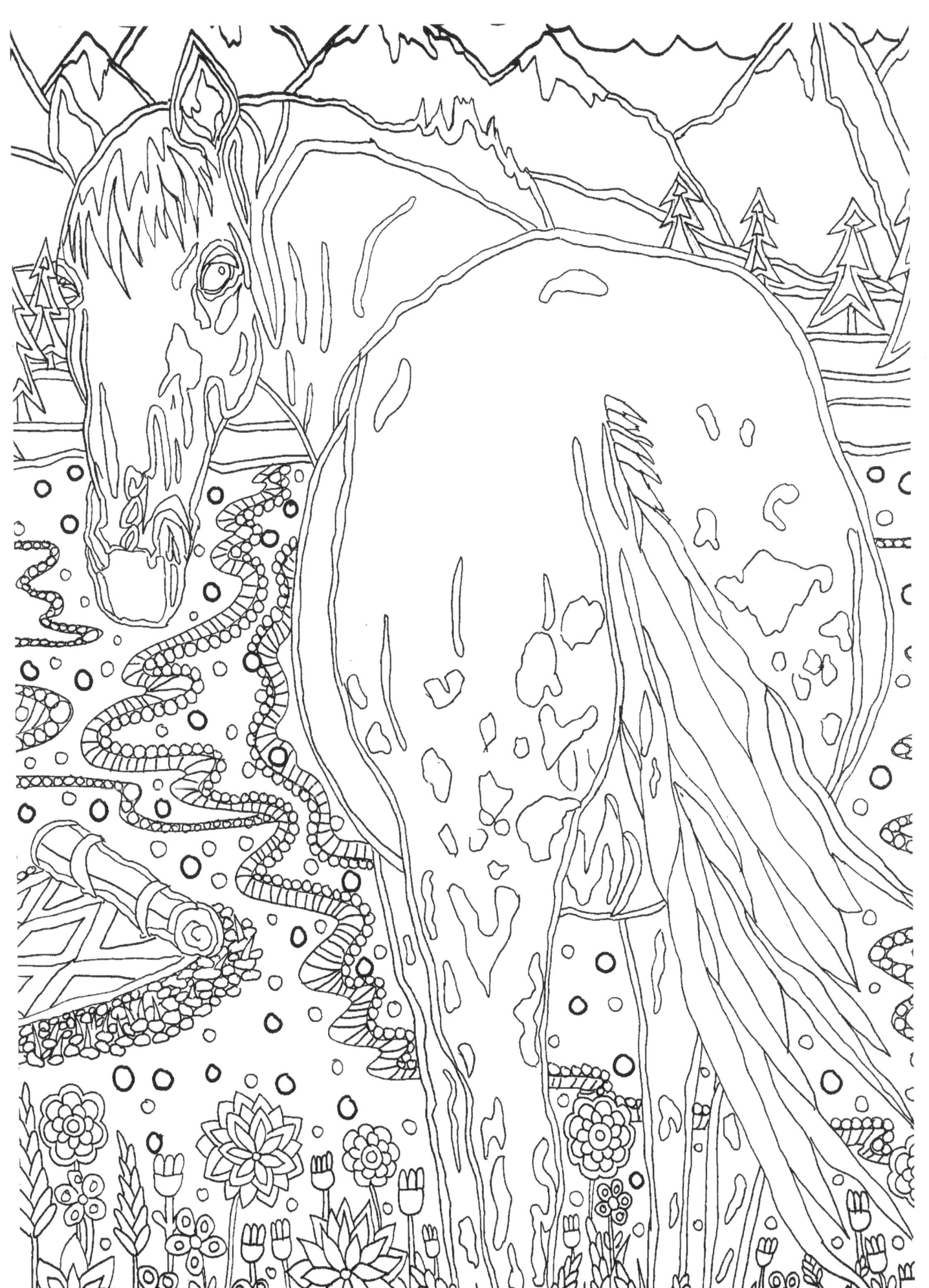

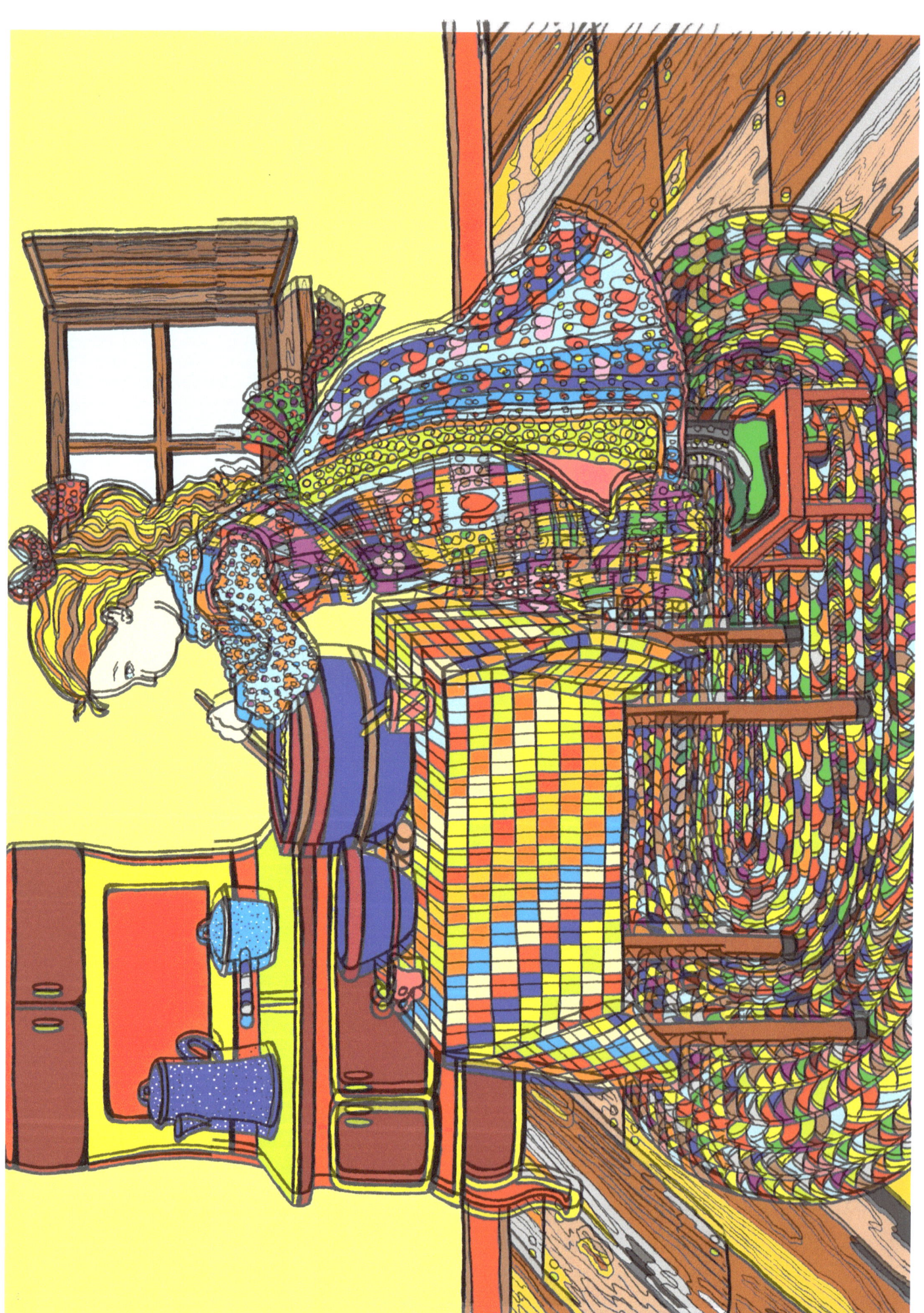

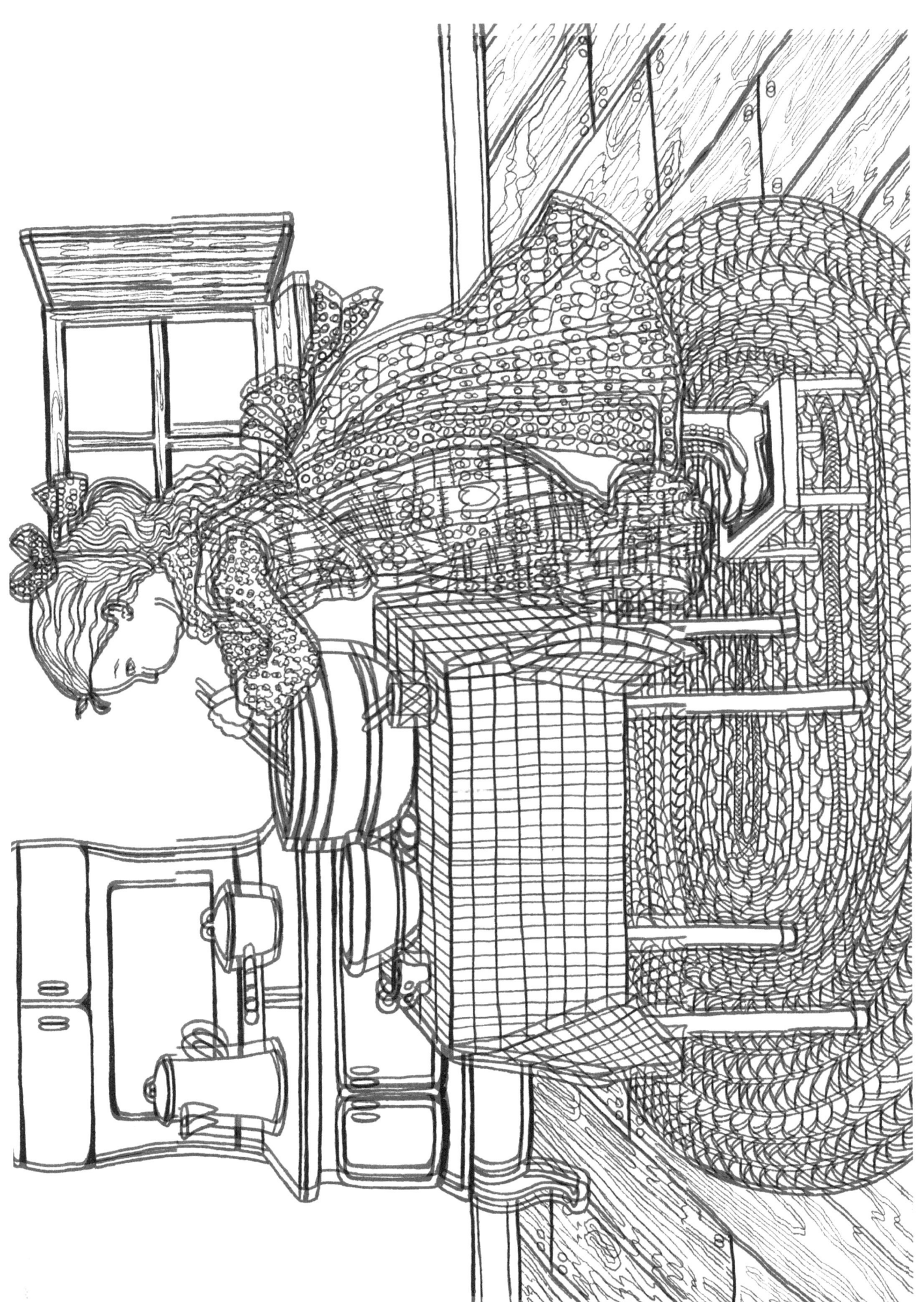

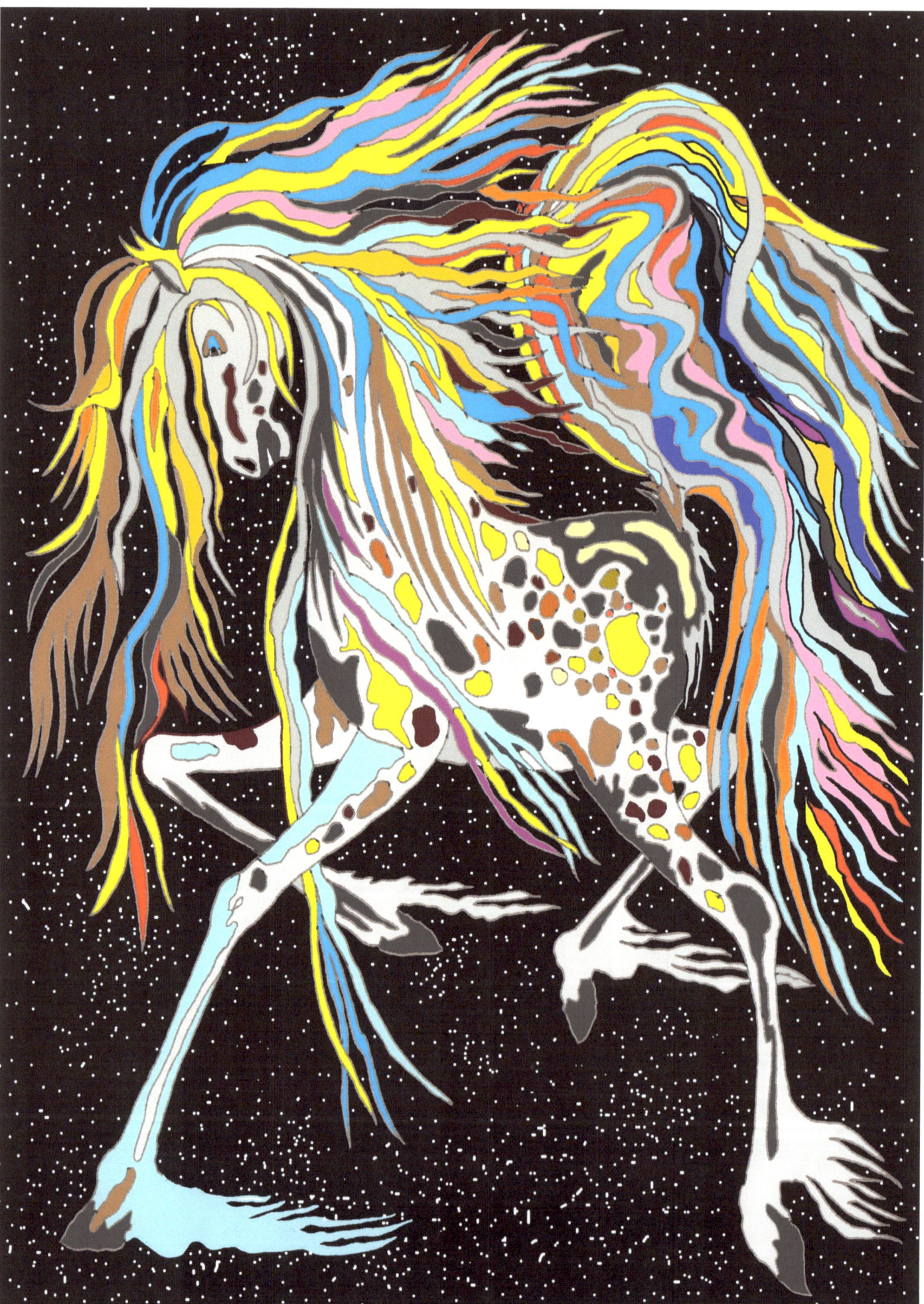

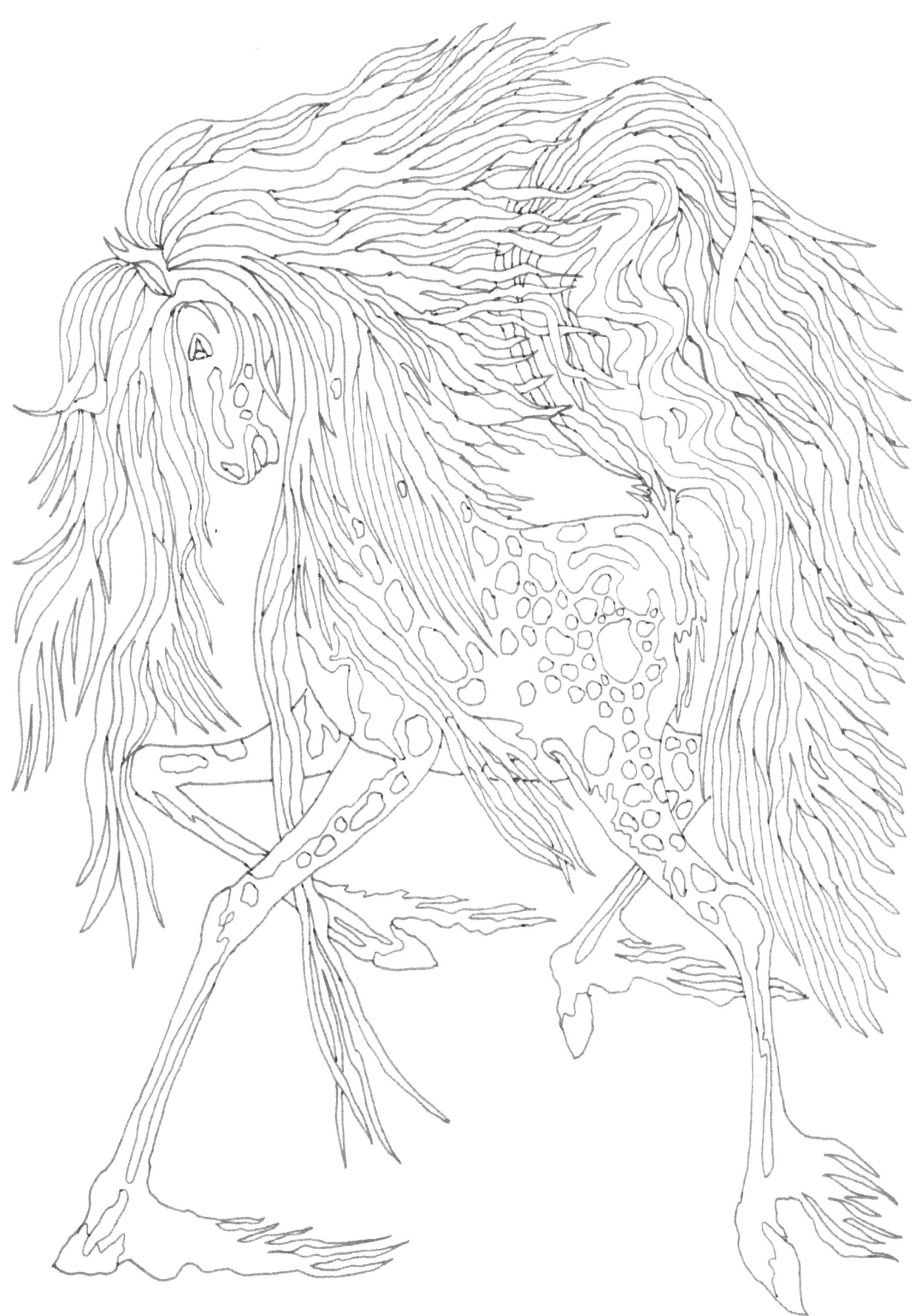

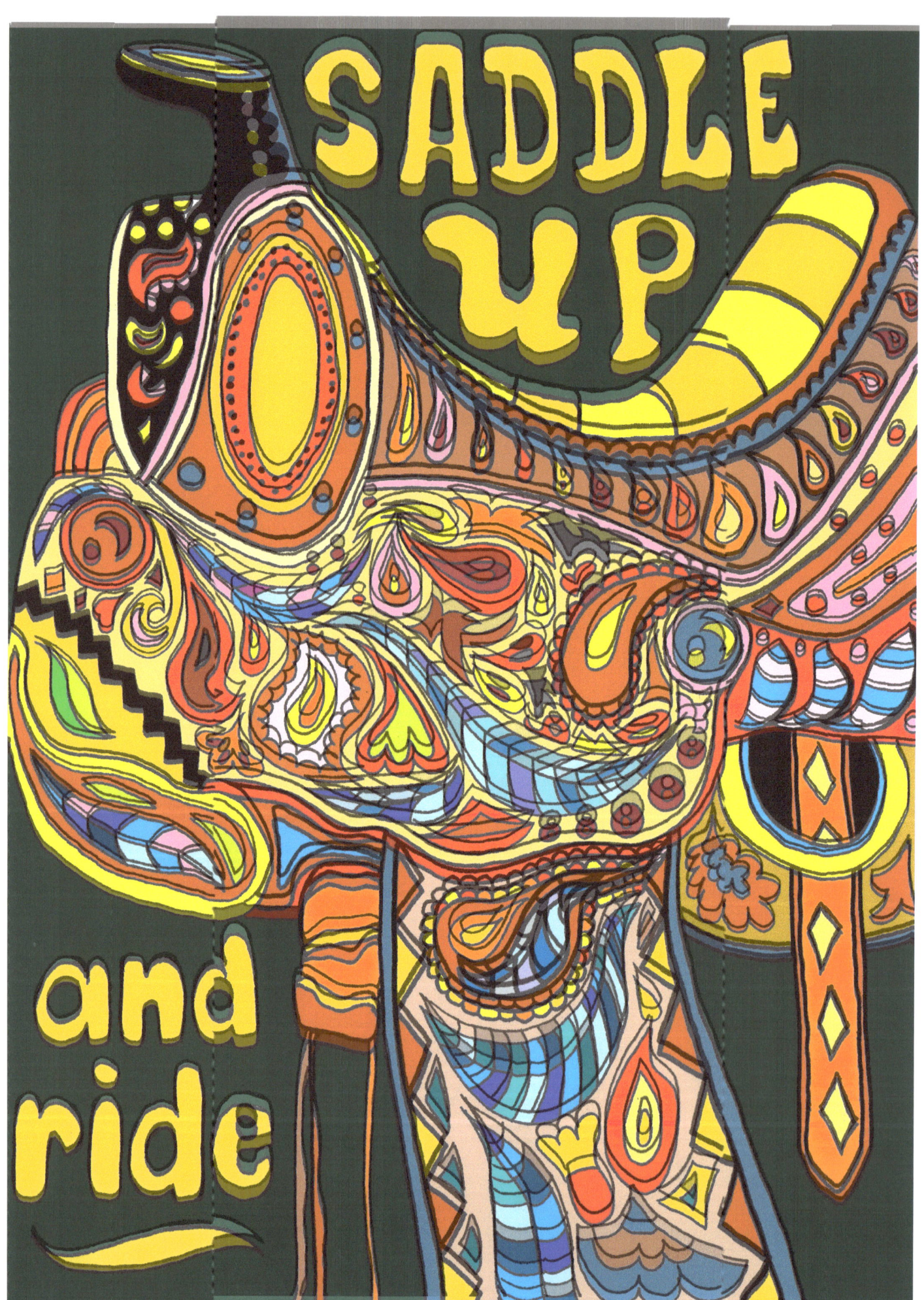

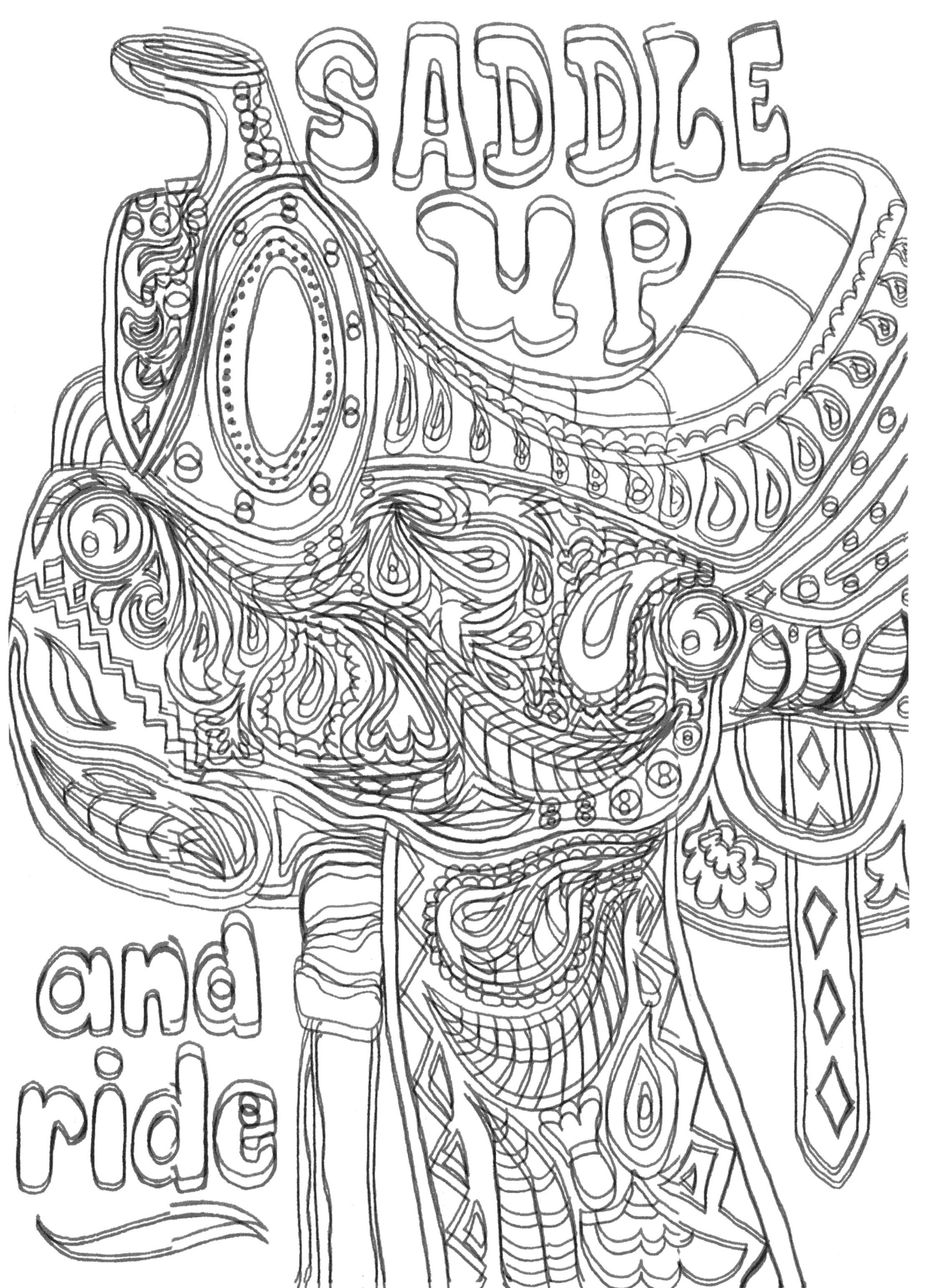

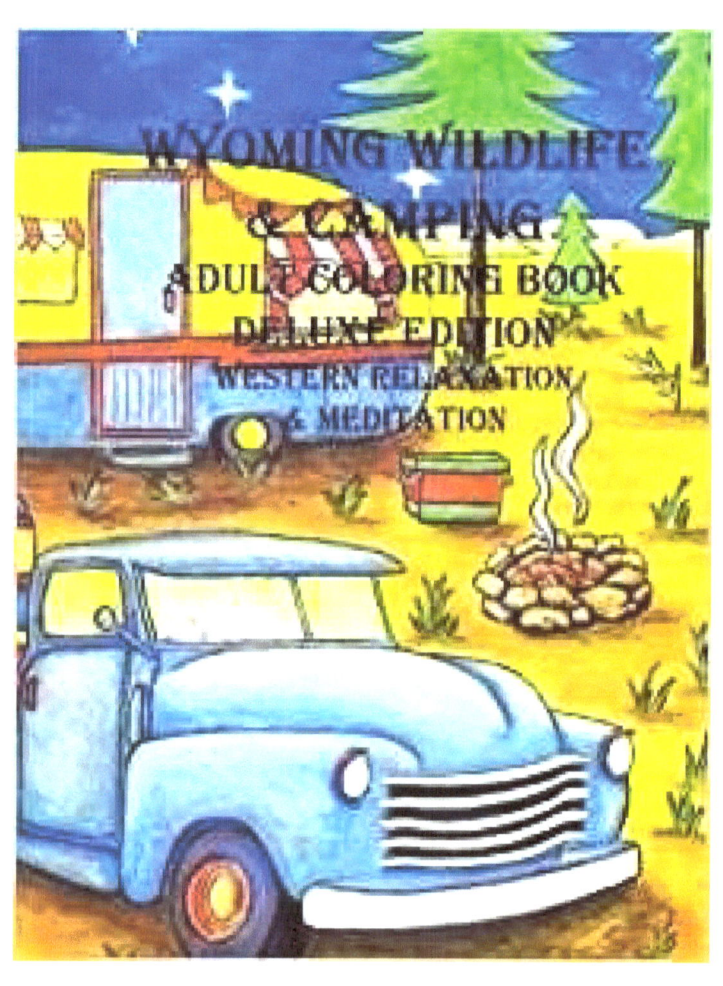
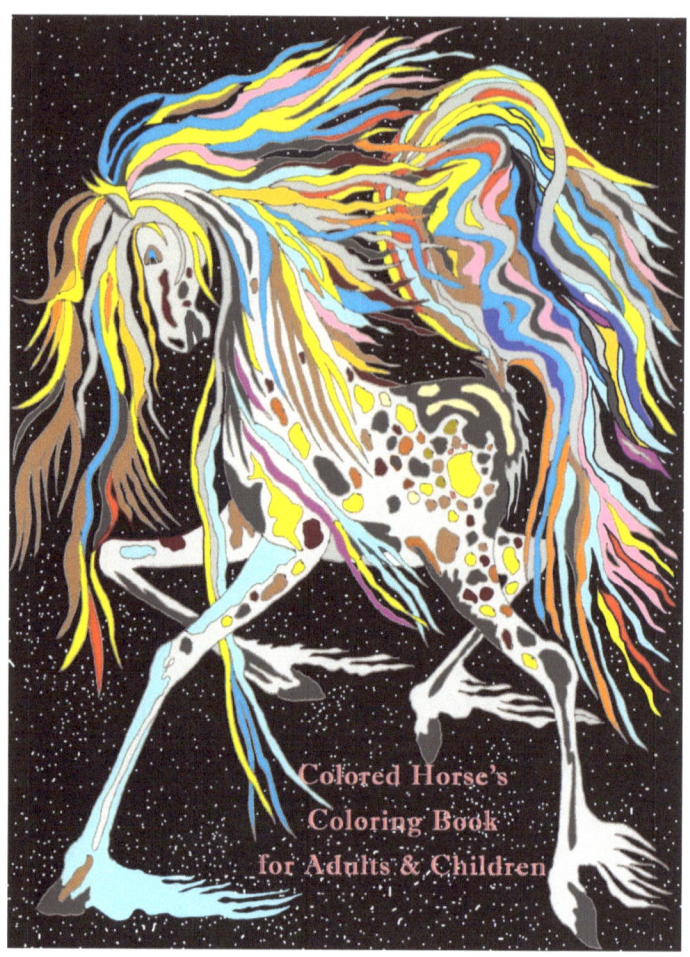
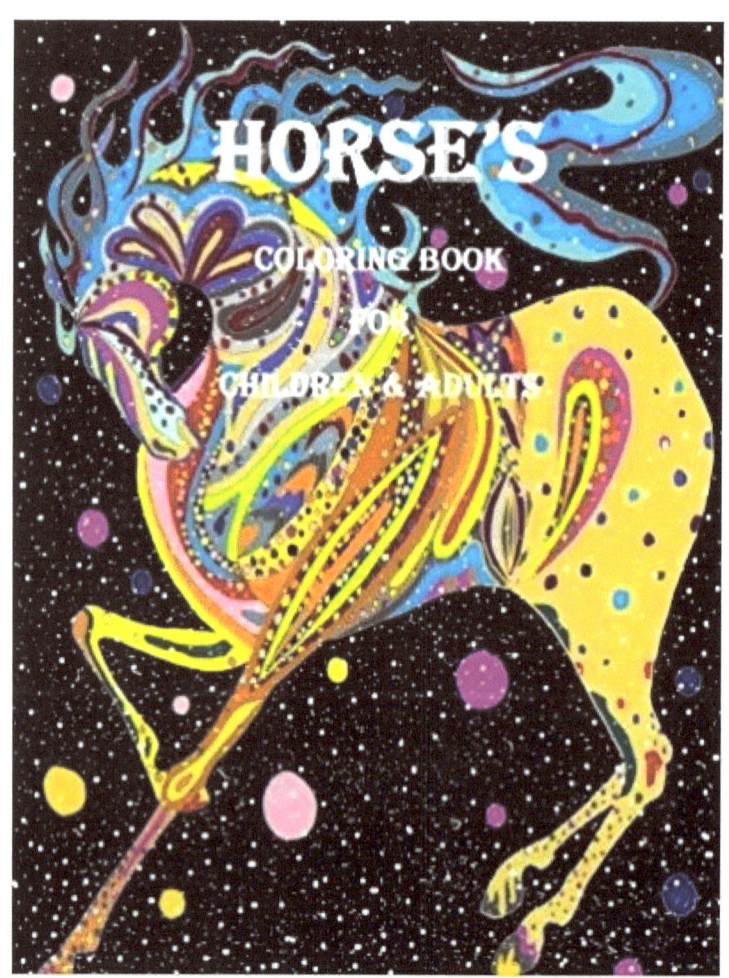
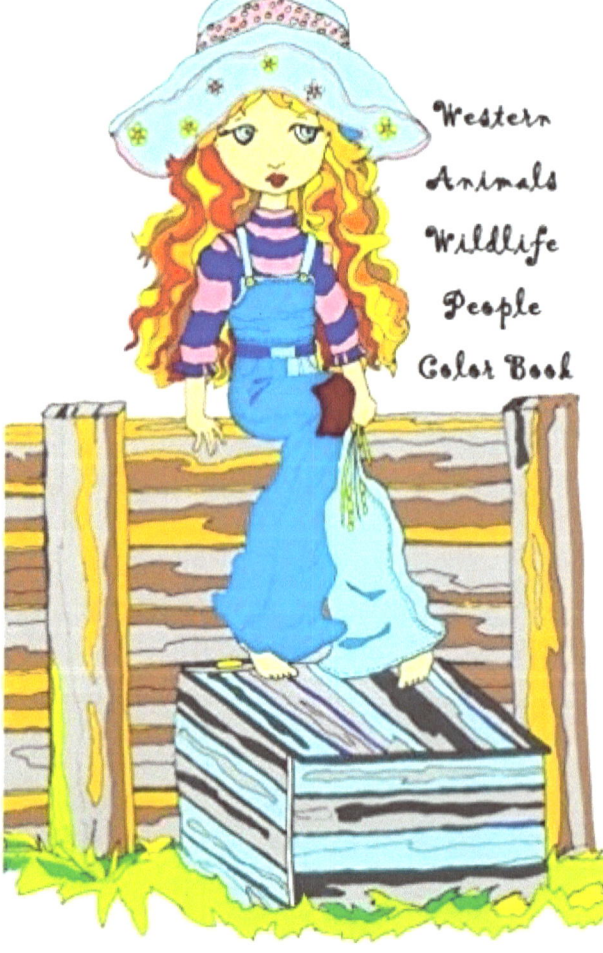

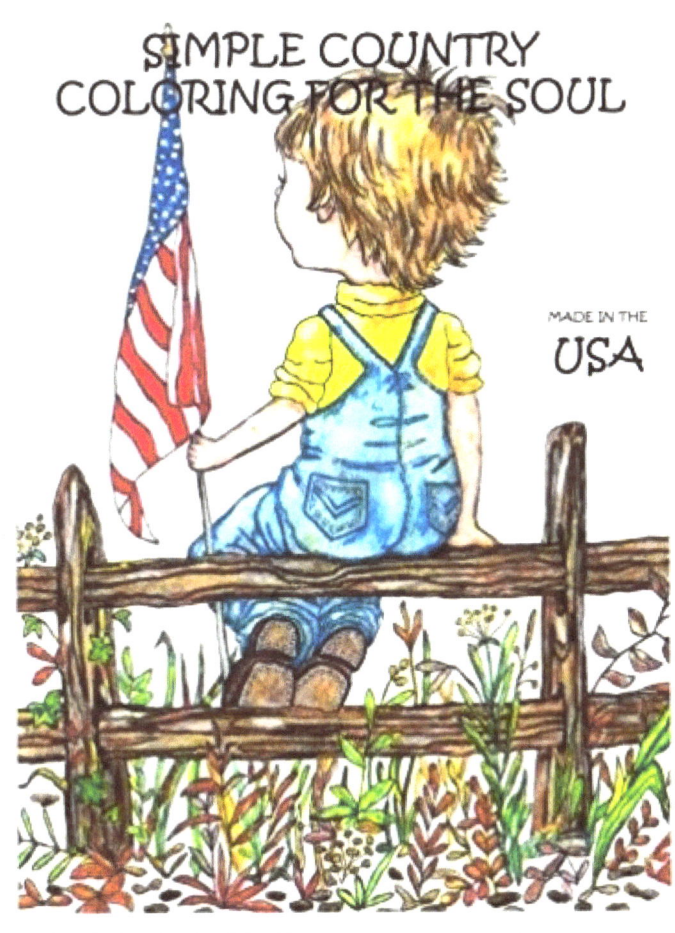
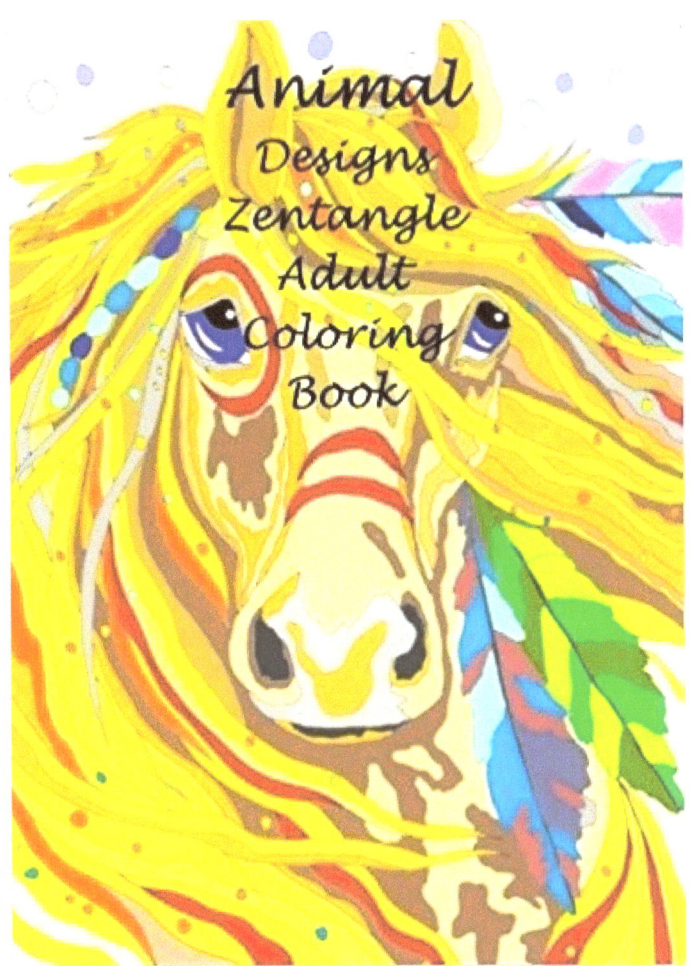
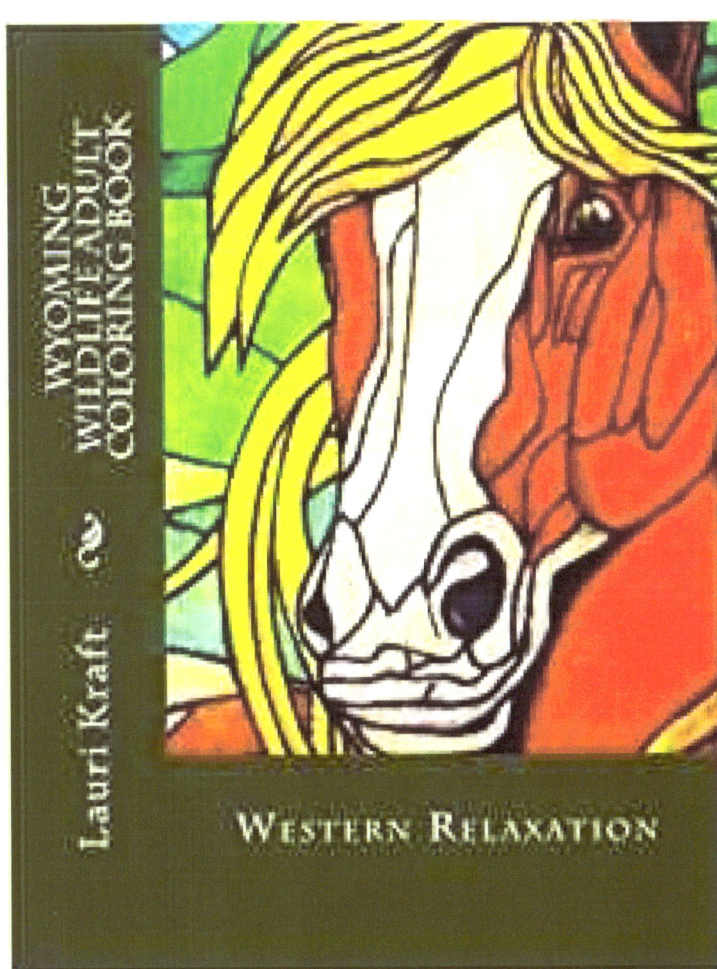
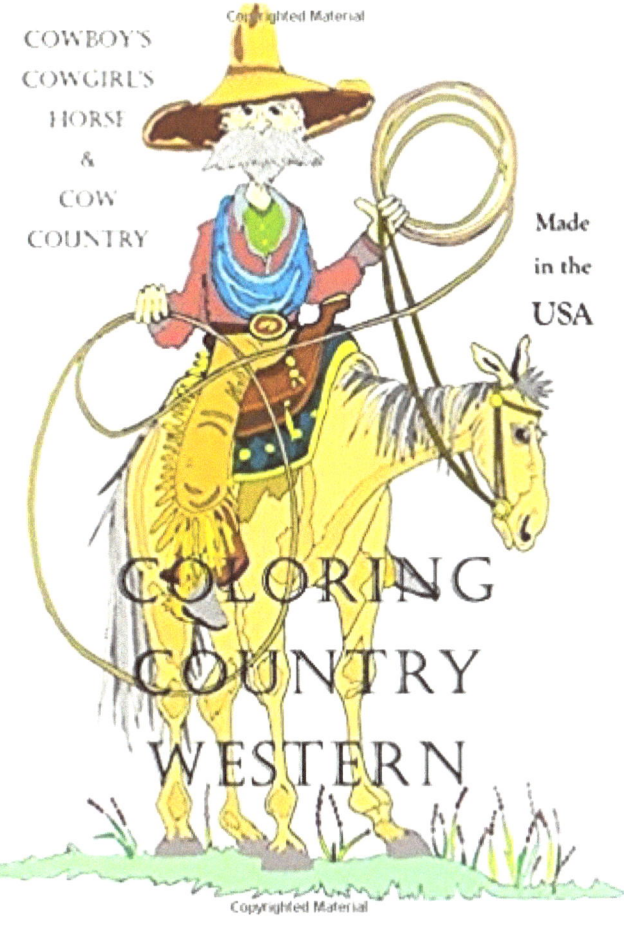

www.ingramcontent.com/pod-product-compliance
Lightning Source LLC
Chambersburg PA
CBHW051918210526

45473CB00006B/2054